Ten Steps
to Breaking the 200 Barrier

Ten Steps
to Breaking
the 200 Barrier

A Church Growth Strategy

by

Bill M. Sullivan

Beacon Hill Press of Kansas City
Kansas City, Missouri

Copyright 1988
by Beacon Hill Press of Kansas City

7/90

ISBN: 083-411-223X

Printed in the
United States of America

Cover: Royce Ratcliff

10 9 8 7 6 5 4 3

L

To C. Peter Wagner,
peerless teacher,
who opened my "church growth eyes"

Contents

Preface

In 1976 I met John Wimber at the airport in Asheville, N.C. It was the beginning of a consulting relationship with Fuller Evangelistic Association and a time of learning church growth principles and strategies. In one of the many sessions we enjoyed together, John made a statement that was the beginning of a fascinating study for me. He said, almost in passing, "We know that there is an 'invisible barrier' that churches face in attempting to grow from 150 to 250." My mental radar locked in on that idea, and I began to research and study the factors that might be involved.

This book represents only a marker on the road and is by no means indicative of reaching the final destination. While it is based on research of 29 churches that actually broke the barrier, much more research on the subject needs to be done. This is an initial venture that hopefully will be expanded by students of church growth.

I am indebted not only to John Wimber but also to Win Arn, who invited me to present a seminar on the subject at the 1987 Executive Briefing Seminar, sponsored by the Institute for American Church Growth. Dale Jones and Ken Crow, statistical and evaluative research managers in our office, deserve special thanks for providing data and interpretation. Nina Beegle, our office editor, deserves the credit for making the manuscript readable. My secretary, Shelli Mann, typed the manuscript and its revisions innumerable times. She deserves special thanks.

A three-year planning calendar that directs the logistics of implementation will be available from the publisher.

Many will find it a helpful tool in launching the thrust to break the 200 barrier.

Perhaps nothing is so desperately needed as something to help that giant majority of churches that never grow beyond an attendance of 150. If even a small percentage of them break the 200 barrier, it would represent an evangelistic advance that would number in the millions! That's something to think about.

INTRODUCTION

Break the Barrier?

Some very interesting statistics have come out of church growth research. One of the most startling is the discovery that most churches in America are small, not just in the smaller denominations but in mainline denominations as well. That probably surprises most people. They're accustomed to seeing imposing church structures on the corners of prominent intersections in larger cities, and several fairly significant church buildings in the middle of small towns. People probably thought a church was not sizable unless it had about 500 members, but they didn't realize how few churches in America actually were that large.

It was Lyle Schaller who first stated that at least half the churches in America average less than 75 in attendance on

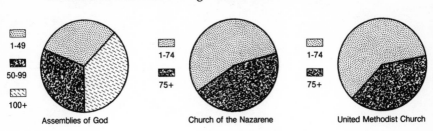

1-49	1-74	1-74
50-99	75+	75+
100+		
Assemblies of God	Church of the Nazarene	United Methodist Church

Fig. 1

11

Sunday morning. That was not a membership statistic but an attendance figure. The three charts in fig. 1 reflect this condition.

It was even more surprising to have Mr. Schaller explain a few years later that while half of the churches in America average less than 75, the most frequent size is only 40.

Researching the small church phenomenon of one denomination revealed that most of the churches were in the "under 50" category. It appeared that the first numerical growth barrier the churches encountered was 50. It was surprising that the barrier would be so low, but the research corroborated Schaller's statement that average attendance in the typical church is in the 40s. This forces the admission that most churches in America are truly small.

Why? Does God prefer small churches? If we interpret church attendance statistics the way sociologists generally interpret research projects, we will conclude the need to have small churches because that's what we have the most of. That's what people appear to prefer. To paraphrase Abraham Lincoln's famous statement about common people, God must love small churches because He made so many of them.

But another statistic affects interpretation. While most churches are small, the greater percentage of attendance is in larger churches. Carl Dudley, in *Making the Small Church Effective*, interprets this as clear indication that people actually prefer larger churches. This is illustrated in the following pie chart.

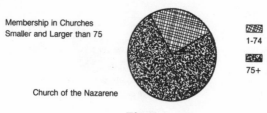

Membership in Churches
Smaller and Larger than 75

1-74

75+

Church of the Nazarene

Fig. 2

12

Some church growth authorities believe that people prefer the control they experience in a smaller church to getting lost in the crowd of a large church. Control of a church sometimes occurs through a primary group. A primary group, typically 12 to 15 people, generally forms to enable people to relate to the larger society. Traditionally the extended family has been a primary group. Frequently smaller churches are primary groups.

Every church has a periphery of people who, though not part of the primary group, occasionally attend. These tend to inflate the upper boundaries for primary group churches to perhaps 50 or 60.

But the prevalence of the small church is more than just a primary-group situation. The small church exists because, beyond a certain size, it is difficult for people to know everyone. In a church of 150 or less, most people know each other on a first-name basis. It could be called the "one big, happy family" church. Not everyone has a close relationship to all the others, but they still consider themselves a part of the big, happy family. However, when the family grows beyond 150, a new phenomenon begins to occur. Individuals can no longer know most of the people in the church.

A pastor speaking at the 75th anniversary of a church recalled a time in the growth history of the congregation that they began to complain about feeling like strangers because of all the new people. The pastor indicated that this anxiety occurred when attendance was between 200 and 300. But beyond 300 he no longer heard much complaint because by then they had made the adjustments that resulted in being a totally different kind of church. That was the result of moving from "one big happy family" (with the intimacy and security that comes from being small enough to watch out for each other and take care of each other) to *an organization*. The most fundamental growth restriction is simply *change*.

Exactly where the numerical barrier is cannot be said

with certainty. In *The Pyramid Principle,* David Womack reports a large national sample showing size-frequency clusters at 50, 90, 120, 180, 230, 290, and 400. In the denomination studied, 80 percent of the churches had fewer than 150 members, and 96 percent of the churches never grew beyond 350. It is perhaps more accurate to speak of a growth barrier in the range of 100 to 300, although several church growth authorities speak of the 200 barrier. If a single arbitrary figure is to be chosen, then 200 is probably a good selection, since it is more convenient to speak of the 200 barrier than a barrier range.

A small church is not a microcosm of a large church but a totally different kind of organization. Just as you would not want to change from being the person you are to being someone else, neither does a church want to give up the family atmosphere to become an organization. As a matter of fact, the very word has an unfriendly sound. Some pastors and laypersons consider organization a necessary evil. It would be wonderful if everything were purely spiritual!

But the realities are that growth, evangelism, and the expansion of the church depend as much on a leader's ability to develop an expansive infrastructure as on any other factor except prayer. The ability to organize to meet people's needs is more important than creativity in program design. In fact, one of the reasons most churches remain small is that organization and administration for growth are not introduced early enough in their development. Of course, no organization can ever compensate for a lack of evangelism, but much of the fruit of evangelism is lost because the church is inadequately organized to assimilate new converts. The church that grows beyond the 200 barrier is the church that decides to minister to its people in a comprehensive organization rather than a family-type fellowship.

But this raises a question. Is it desirable to try to break through the 200 barrier? Several factors must be considered when facing that challenge. What is the demographic situation of the community? A community of 1,500 to 3,000 people, or even 10,000 people, that is static or declining and is adequately churched, may not be the best place to try to break the barrier. That is something each pastor must decide. What is the average-size church in your town? In the thinking of your people, what number constitutes average size?

A pastor must also consider how long he plans to stay at the church. If the church increases to 300 and he moves, will his successor allow it to decline back below the barrier?

Still another consideration is, what kind of debt commitment will significant growth require?

Ultimately, however, the desirability of breaking the barrier hinges on the question, "Do people prefer larger churches?" Today the preference for larger churches seems greater than in the past, though it may not be possible to accurately determine the preferences of the past. Television has exposed people to superchurches. The anonymity of society in general may have caused people to prefer larger groups rather than smaller ones where accountability is greater.

However, bear in mind that any church that grows larger, sustains growth, and at the same time ministers to its people will have within it small accountability groups. A large proportion of the people will be absorbed into some type of group. So it's not that people escape accountability when they attend a large church, it is only that it is organized differently. Of course, larger churches contain many people who are simply spectators, but churches of 60 or 70 also have spectators, though the percentage may be smaller.

Another factor to consider in deciding whether or not to break the 200 barrier is the desirability of starting a new church. Would it not be better to make plans for another church or even several other churches over a period of time? Could the people be served better this way? Could they maintain the intimacy, security, and accountability of the smaller church and still experience the excitement of growth?

Actually, this is not an either/or situation. The realities are that the church may be better able to spawn a new church if they first grow beyond the 200 barrier. Below the 200 barrier, they may never see the need for starting a new church.

The general desire for church growth and the preference toward larger churches indicates the desirability of breaking the 200 barrier. The question is how. The following 10 steps describe how to break the barrier.

SUMMARY

- Most churches in America are small, the most frequent size being 40; however, the greater percentage of people attend large churches (250 or more).
- There are reasons why churches stay small, and frequency clusters that indicate points at which growth is arrested, but the evidence is strong that these growth barriers should be broken through and reasons for nongrowth overcome.
- Breaking the barriers should be a question not so much of *when* but of *how*.

STEP 1

Examine Your Motive

Why do you want to break the barrier? Unless the motive for growth is to proclaim the Good News to those who are lost and see them saved by the power of Christ, you will be working from an inadequate motive.

Does the motivation come from a desire to pastor a larger church? If so, you have a really big job on your hands. Even if you're an exceptionally gifted and winsome person, with that motive you're going to have a difficult time making a church grow. Undoubtedly it has happened; probably there are some places it is happening right now, and it will likely happen in the future, but that is not the best motivation for growth.

Someone may say, "Well, you're simply advocating a spiritual motivation in order to grow, but growing a big church is still what you want to do. The motivation is still impure." But the motivation is not to grow a bigger church. The motivation is to obey God's call to *tell the whole world the Good News.* There is no such thing as having a vision only for the lost in your town. The assignment that Christ gave to His followers was to reach the whole world. Start at Jerusalem, but don't stop there; work outward. The pastor who wants only to reach his local community or city does not really have the mission perspective of a true disciple.

This is not promotion for overseas mission; it's a realistic appraisal of the Great Commission. We don't like to believe that people are lost. It would be more comfortable to be a universalist, and it would certainly reduce the responsibility. But the Bible will not permit that. It prevents us from believing that everyone is going to be saved someday, someway, and it's very plain in declaring that some people will be lost. The sobering message of the Bible is that those who are sent to preach will be held responsible if they fail to warn the lost. Therefore, thinking about breaking the 200 barrier forces us to ask ourselves, "Why do we want to break it?" So we can have more people? That may be good, but that is not a strong enough motivation.

Motive has not been properly dealt with until the difficulty of being objective is considered. It is too easy to question the motive of another, but actually it is impossible to know his thoughts. This is certainly true in regard to growth. One pastor may seek growth in the church and claim it is because he wants to see souls saved. Another, looking on, may declare that the preacher simply has a desire for personal advancement. It is well-nigh impossible to determine which person is correct. Even when a person prays searchingly, it is difficult for him to know his own heart. Most of us have experienced times when we believed we were doing what was right but later wondered if we were carried away under the emotion of the moment. Religious experience and spiritual intimacy are wonderful, but they must always be subjected to the judgment of the Word of God. Of course, in areas of specific guidance and personal motivation, the Bible cannot be expected to arbitrate; so even though we pray, we may not know our true motivation.

The natural tendency of the human heart is to cover up any proclivity that might be considered selfish. A variety of rationalizations are used to escape responsibility for impure motives.

People may say, "You're just trying to feather your own nest," or "You're just trying to get your name in the district newsletter," or "You're just trying to build a larger church so you can get a bigger salary." If your motivation is reaching the lost, those kinds of charges will roll off you like water off a duck's back, because you know in your soul that you are seeking the lost.

It is easy to be superficial in the area of motives, just as it is easy to be superficial in the areas of action. Pacificism and inactivity do not necessarily indicate pure motivation, nor does aggressive, energetic action necessarily indicate personal ambition. We must not allow either Satan or well-intentioned people to cause us to shrink back from being aggressive evangels for Christ. At the same time, we must not allow the desire for personal satisfaction and ambitious fulfillment to be the driving motivation of our ministry.

We say to ministers, "If you can do anything besides preach, don't preach. But if you have to preach to save your soul, then preach." That's the only kind of conviction that will hold you steady in the ministry when the going gets rough. The realization that we are responsible for the souls of men and women will keep us going when we run into resistance to growth.

Now, suppose you privately conclude in searching your soul that the truth is, you want to pastor a bigger church. The truth is, you want to be in the top 10, or the top whatever. You don't *want* to feel that way about it, but God help you, that is the way you feel! What are you going to do about that?

A passion for souls comes out of prayer. And while we don't use prayer simply to help us grow a great church, prayer is foundational to any kind of ministry. You don't have to be known as the most prayerful preacher on the district. You don't have to spend hours and hours in prayer just because some other ministers do, but the effective pastor does need a regular, consistent, substantial prayer life. And that prayer life needs to deal with the task of ministry.

We need to pray about the lost, "O God, what do You expect me to do?" A burden for the lost comes out of prayer.

You can stand on the street corner and watch the masses of people go by, and you may feel some empathy for them, but you'll also feel overwhelmed by the magnitude of trying to reach those people for Christ. It is disheartening to realize how many billions of people are unsaved. The Bible says we're supposed to win the lost, and we try to act on that. But the necessary emotional content will not be there until we get down on our faces before God and grapple with it in prayer, then rise from that place with some kind of conviction that God wants the lost found and the sinful saved, that He is "not willing that any should perish, but that all should come to repentance" (2 Pet. 3:9), and that He wants *you* and *me* to reach them. So we go out with a burning conviction, not just a desire for denominational or personal aggrandizement.

When you reach this point, it doesn't really matter whether or not you have the largest church in town. You just want to reach everyone possible for Christ, and you know in your heart and mind that if you do, the chances are excellent that your church is going to grow. Now, if you're going to reach them, and if you're going to grow, and if you're going to have a wide ministry, your church has to become a different kind of church, but that won't just happen because your motive is right.

We don't pray because we just roll out of bed and our knees hit the floor and we think, While I'm down here, I'll just pray. We pray because we have a very definite discipline in our lives. Church growth happens the same way. Your church will grow because you have a very definite discipline for growth. We are so accustomed to spiritualizing things that we think growth is miraculous—that if God wants us to grow, we'll grow, and if He doesn't want us to grow, we're not going to grow. I have yet to meet a person who states, "We're growing, but I just have to be honest with you, we're not doing a thing to cause it." I do meet pastors who admit, "I don't know at this point exactly what it is we're doing that is causing growth," and I meet pastors who acknowledge, as they should, "God is helping us to grow," but I've never met one who said, "We're growing even though I'm not doing anything." They all declare, "I'm working my head off, and several of the people in my church are working like pile drivers, too."

When you examine your motives and pray until the drive of your life is to reach the lost, you must follow up with some intentionality. One of the real dualisms in life for the Christian is, "How much depends on God and how much depends on me?" The best anyone has ever been able to resolve that is by suggesting, "Trust like everything depends on God and work like everything depends on you." That has to be incorporated into the plan and the effort to grow. You are doing this because it is essential to the primary task of ministering, and it is the real desire of your heart to reach the lost. Your prayer might be: "And God, if that's not what I want to do, work on me until that *is* what I want to do. Work on me until the fundamental motive of my work for growth is to see the lost found, redeemed, and transformed."

Probably the best way of determining true motivation is by watching action and practice and then evaluating results. Was the action and practice in the direction of bringing recognition to the person? Was the result of the action the advancement of the pastor? Did it result in the salvation of souls? Did, in fact, the church grow, or was it simply a stepping-stone for a minister's career advancement?

The same procedure can also be applied to the pastor

who insists that numerical growth is not a noble enough goal. Generally such a person will indicate that it is more important to grow in spiritual depth than it is to grow numerically. Surely no one would question the importance of spiritual growth or of discipleship training in the church, but there is no way to determine the true motive in this kind of commitment. Are the people, in fact, deepening in spiritual things? Is the congregation maturing? Is there a new hunger and thirst for truth and for the Word of God? Is the church growing spiritually, even though it is not growing numerically?

Jesus said, "Ye have not chosen me, but I have chosen you, and ordained you, that ye should go and bring forth fruit, and that your fruit should remain" (John 15:16). The issue is not activity or inactivity but a question of whether or not the fruit, claimed as the basis for motivation, actually was produced as the result of the activity. Only God can determine the driving force of our ministry.

As we examine our motivation for wanting to break through the 200 barrier, let us be careful that we do not come to inaccurate conclusions. Let us not deceive ourselves; let us not be intimidated by others. Let us seek, rather, to open our hearts and lives to the full will of God.

SUMMARY

- Motivation for church growth must emerge from the desire to bring lost souls to a knowledge of Christ as Savior, beginning in our Jerusalem and reaching to the uttermost parts of the earth. Personal satisfaction and ambitious fulfillment are not sufficient motivation.

- Pacifism and inactivity do not necessarily indicate pure motivation, nor does aggressive, energetic action necessarily indicate personal ambition.

- A regular, consistent, substantial prayer life that deals with the task of ministry will get the pastor beyond desire for denominational or personal aggrandizement and build in the heart a passion for souls.

- When you examine your motives and pray until the drive of your life is to reach the lost, you must follow up with some intentionality.

- Motivation can be determined by watching action and practice, then evaluating results.

STEP 2

Intensify Your Praying

One of the remarkable realities of Jesus' life was His dependence upon prayer. His ministry appeared to be based on His prayer life. Repeatedly we are told that Jesus went alone to pray. Before He selected His 12 apostles, He spent the night in prayer. Prayer was an important aspect of Jesus' ministry.

Prayer must also be a vital dimension of the pastor's life. He cannot depend alone upon training, literary resources, or natural ability. The work that he has been called to do demands far more than human resources can possibly provide. He must have divine help. "Were not the right Man on our side," writes Martin Luther, "our striving would be losing." Without Christ to give us strength in our ministry, we cannot hope to succeed in the work He has called us to do. Any hope whatever that we will be able to build Christ's Church without Christ himself will be completely in vain. Any thought of breaking the 200 barrier and building a great church for the glory of God will be wishful thinking without a vital prayer link with God. It is difficult to explain this, for it does not submit to reason, but it is a reality that has been demonstrated beyond doubt.

It is easy to fall under the accusation that calling for prayer is a utilitarian means of accomplishing a selfish end, but the person who makes that accusation is overlooking the tremendous power of prayer. Prayer changes people. When we pray, we begin to realize our responsibility to be obedient to our Lord. As He asked in His own ministry, "Why do you call me, 'Lord, Lord,' and do not do what I say?" (Luke 6:46). Prayer inevitably brings us to realize that God wants us to reach the lost, to find people who are outside the fold. God wants us to be active in the building of His Church. A strong personal prayer life will effect a transformation of life that will fix our attention on the concerns that move the heart of God.

Personal prayer, however, will not be enough in the long run to build His Church; it will also require corporate prayer. Not every individual member in the church must pray earnestly, but there must be a concerted group effort in prayer that God will help the pastor and church accomplish what He has called them to do. In praying this way, we are seeking not our own desires but rather divine energy to do what He has called us to do, what He has commissioned us to do, what He has charged us to do. We cannot do it in our own strength. We must have divine power and intervention. Something happens when God's people get together and pray. It is more than group psychology. It is rather His response, "Where two or three come together in my name, there am I with them" (Matt. 18:20). Probably every pastor has observed the phenomenon that when God's people get together and pray, wonderful things happen.

This corporate prayer must be more than occasional and spasmodic. It must be consistent; it must be intense; it must be patient. There is something about the time lag between our prayers and the answers that come that tends to weed out those who are not really committed to sincere prayer. Praying requires so much energy and takes so much time before results accrue that those with shallow commitments generally give up before they ever realize any true benefits. So the church that is faithful to its call and obedient to the Lord in moving out to reach the lost and bringing them into the Kingdom must keep on praying until the answer comes.

While it is vitally important that both pastor and people pray, they must also work. Prayer is not a substitute for work, it is the foundation for work. Out of prayer comes holy work and holy effectiveness in work. Together they bring dramatic results. As I understand the New Testament, we are not asked to pray until God does the work for us; we are rather exhorted to pray until God gives us the strength and the power to do the work He has called us to do. So intensify your personal and congregational praying, while you move out to work and to win the lost. Break the barrier! Hundreds and hundreds of people will be saved, sanctified, and incorporated into the life of the church.

Jesus declared, "As long as it is day, we must do the work of him who sent me. Night is coming, when no one can work" (John 9:4). There is always a time limit on our opportunities. Realizing that the time is short, we must pray and then get on with the work, never stopping the praying, but always working in the power of the Spirit that comes through prayer. This is the only way that praying without ceasing truly makes sense. We continue to pray while we are working.

When I took church growth training at Fuller Theological Seminary, I met a young man who was a quick learner and a very articulate spokesman. Six months later we both returned for a second church growth seminar. At that time we shared some of the things that had been going on in our lives following our initial training. I well remember that this young pastor indicated he had developed in his church a PPCG

Club. He had all the people talking about the PPCG Club. Only those who agreed to keep the club requirements were allowed to know what the letters stood for. They stood for "Please Pray for Church Growth." Today that young man is nationally engaged as a very effective church growth consultant across denominational lines. He understood that the very foundation of church growth, or any great work for God, is prayer. If you are to break the 200 barrier in your church, you must intensify your own praying and the praying of your people. Your heart must cry out for them to "please pray for church growth!"

SUMMARY

- Breaking the 200 barrier and building a church for the glory of God will be wishful thinking without a vital prayer link with God.

- *Personal Prayer*
  A strong personal prayer life will effect a transformation of life that will fix the attention on the concerns that move the heart of God.

- *Corporate Prayer*
  Building His Church will also require corporate prayer for divine power, strength, and intervention.

- Prayer must be consistent, intense, patient.

- Prayer must be accompanied by work. Out of prayer comes holy work and holy effectiveness that bring dramatic results.

STEP 3

Increase Your Faith

The disciples asked the Lord, "Increase our faith!" (Luke 17:5). The Bible defines faith in many and varied ways. E. C. Blackman, in the *Interpreter's Dictionary of the Bible,* defines faith as "belief in something, or trust in some person." Faith could be the belief that God created the world—creation faith. Or it could be belief in God's plan of salvation—creedal faith. Or it could be trust in Christ for salvation—saving faith. It could be trust in God for continual strength and help in living the Christian life and responding to day-by-day challenges.

In addition to these common understandings of the meaning and application of faith, the New Testament contains another concept of faith: "the gift of faith." This is what W. T. Purkiser defines as "mountain-moving faith." The best explanation of mountain-moving faith, or the gift of faith, that I have found is in Elmer Towns's *Stepping Out on Faith.* In chapter 14, he differentiates between three uses of the gift of faith. The first he calls *instrumental,* using the gift of faith to do God's work, much as one might use the Bible to preach the

Good News. The second is what he calls *insight* or vision, the gift of faith to see what God wants done. I suspect that there are many ministers who believe that knowing what God wants done in the church is their responsibility. They consider it a pastoral prerogative rather than an insightful use of the gift of faith. But the ability to know what God wants to do in the life of a church requires more than faith for daily living. It necessitates the gift of faith.

Towns's third understanding of the gift of faith is what he describes as *interventional.* By this he means using the gift of faith to move God to act on behalf of some specific ministry. He sees the interventional use of the gift of faith as most important for church growth. He describes the application of the gift of faith in this way: (1) announcing a solution to problems facing the ministry, and (2) setting goals, or announcing specific plans for the ministry.[1]

This threefold interpretation of the gift of faith can make an important contribution to church growth understanding. It is easy to be negative about claims of extraordinary faith. There have been so many overly zealous, yet well-intentioned, ministers who attempted things for God that they were unable to complete. Although they had announced that this was unquestionably the leading and the will of God, the plan failed and collapsed. Both clergy and laity, observing those experiences, are inclined to speak disdainfully about mountain-moving faith. Yet it is a biblical concept, and it should not be ignored or neglected. It is important to understand the proper use of mountain-moving faith, and Elmer Towns has given us that.

You may respond, "I don't think I have the gift of faith. I'm just not able to believe God for great miracles or to do spectacular things in my ministry." Or you may say, "I would like to have the gift of faith, but I have to be realistic about it. I don't believe that I possess it, or if I possess it, it certainly isn't very strong. I need to pray as the disciples asked the

Lord, 'Increase our faith!' or as the man who brought his son to Jesus to be healed, 'I do believe; help me overcome my unbelief!'" (Luke 17:5 and Mark 9:24).

Permit me to make six suggestions that, though simple, should help you increase the measure of faith that God has given you.

Read about faith in Bible passages like Matthew 21 and 22; Mark 9:23-24; 11:23-24; Luke 17:5; Acts 3:16; Hebrews 11:1. Read about Abraham, whose life was one great venture of faith. Read about his intervention for his nephew, Lot. Read about Moses, who repeatedly moved the heart of God on behalf of the Israelites. Read also about Paul in the New Testament, who moved out on faith to do mighty works for God. You won't have any difficulty finding mountain-moving faith passages.

Read about faith in faith-inspiring books. I would suggest biographies and autobiographies of great people of faith like George Müller. The story of his life is remarkable, and few question the genuineness of his mountain-moving faith. There are many biographies and autobiographies of people "who through faith conquered kingdoms, administered justice, and gained what was promised; who shut the mouths of lions, quenched the fury of the flames, and escaped the edge of the sword; whose weakness was turned to strength; and who became powerful in battle and routed foreign armies" (Heb. 11:33-34).

Read the stories of great churches. In recent years, many books have appeared on the market that tell the story of a particular church, and how the faith and vision of the pastor resulted in tremendous ministry. As you read those faith-inspiring books, you will discover your own faith being strengthened and encouraged.

Look for examples of mountain-moving faith. Watch for those people whose lives indicate they have the gift of faith.

It may be a fellow minister or a layperson in your church. There should be something about that person's faith that reaps rewards. Watch for it. It will challenge your own faith and encourage you to trust God for great victories. Look for instances where great vision has resulted in tremendous accomplishment. The Bible says, "Where there is no vision, the people perish" (Prov. 29:18, KJV). There is an implied corollary, "Where there is vision, God's people are built up in their most holy faith," and it is probably accurate to say that the church also grows.

Listen to people of great faith. When you have opportunity to hear persons whom you know to have great faith, listen to them carefully. What do they have to say about faith? How do they describe mountain-moving faith, and what do they recommend to others in regard to increasing their faith? We are all aware that stories of falsification persist against some who claim to be people of faith. True or not, I cannot say. I only recommend that you listen to people you know to be persons of great faith, whose reputations are of good report.

Ask God to increase your faith as the disciples did as recorded in Luke 17:5. Jesus' response to the disciples' request is interesting. He didn't say, "All right, that's what I was hoping you'd request." There really isn't much indication that He was even delighted. It would seem to us the Lord should have been pleased that the disciples wanted to have more faith, but that was not His response.

On the other hand, He didn't reply, "That's not something you should be asking for." He didn't indicate that it was something beyond them or something too sacred for them to concern themselves with. Instead, He appears to have replied, "It doesn't take much faith to love and forgive people or to move mountains."

Some of the biblical expositors who deal with this passage relate backward to Jesus' demand that they forgive a brother, even if he comes back seven times in the same day requesting forgiveness. Those who look at the passage this way tend to indicate that Jesus is saying, "It isn't more faith you need, but it's the right kind of faith. And if you have the right kind of faith, you will indeed be able to forgive your brother."

Other expositors have indicated that faith is like a mustard seed and, though it is very small, it will grow and flourish into a great garden plant, and in time it will develop into a mighty faith that can even move mountains into the midst of the sea.

But whether it is the right kind of faith or a sufficient faith, it's right to pray about it. If Jesus never intended mountain-moving faith to be a part of the Christian's life, then we might wonder why He brought the subject up and why He referred to it on more than one occasion. So don't hesitate to ask God to increase your faith. After all, He has called you to preach the gospel. He has placed you in your present circumstance, and in all likelihood you need mountain-moving faith to accomplish all that He is calling you to do. So pray as the disciples asked the Lord, "Increase our faith!."

Increasing your faith involves the element of "stepping out on faith." As in most experiences in the Christian life, it is not enough simply to believe; we must act on our belief. We must not only have faith, we must demonstrate our faith by our works. As leaders of the church, not only must we pray that God would work a mighty miracle, but also we must move out in confidence that He will.

Now this is not an exhortation to jump out on faith, which might be a zealous but self-satisfying extravagance. It's easy to get excited about mountain-moving faith and attempt something that God hasn't even talked to you about doing. It's easy to get carried away with selfish dreams of grandeur

32

and do something that is not based in the divine will but in the personal ego.

Neither is it a suggestion to disregard wisdom and hazard other people's futures. Many laypersons are skeptical of a pastor's recommendation to step out on faith because they have previously suffered the consequences of what turned out to be bad judgment rather than genuine faith. This is a delicate area because some minister might say, If the people had really trusted God, what we were trying to accomplish would have come to pass. On the other hand, the laypeople may say, The pastor jumped ship and didn't stay to face the consequences of his action. If his faith had been genuine, he would not have deserted. There is no way to resolve these conflicting perspectives, but they do provide a backdrop against which an appeal for genuine faith may be made. This exhortation to step out on faith is a word of encouragement to seek God's will for your ministry and then simply move out.

It may or may not involve financial risk. Some ministers have increased their credibility in this area by making sure that all the financial risk was their own. Generally, we run into trouble when the financial risk that we are advocating is someone else's.

Mountain-moving faith will certainly involve risk taking. You will probably not accomplish a great work for God until you move into the region of risk. This is the point at which you step out on faith, the place at which you will discover whether your faith has increased or is still severely lacking. But the probability is great that if you have read about faith, if you have looked for examples of mountain-moving faith, if you have listened to people of great faith, and you have asked God to increase your faith, when you step out on faith through the power of the Holy Spirit, a great work will be accomplished.

This is not to say that every pastor must have the gift of faith, although a call to the ministry is a call to leadership, and leaders must depend heavily on the gift of faith. The pastors we call church growth pastors tend to have the gift of faith. The probability is, if you went to any large church in America and became acquainted with the pastor, you'd discover he has the gift of faith.

If you don't have the gift of faith, begin praying for God to increase the measure of your faith until you believe in God's ability to work in this world and in His desire to work through you. You must do that in the conviction that God wants you to reach the lost, and that requires building a great church. And because God is going to help you, you *can* build a great church.

A leader who isn't convinced that God wants to build a great church through him and reach the lost in great numbers will not be helped by any methodology or opportunity. He can be placed in the best growth opportunity in America, and his church won't grow, because a pastor must believe that God has called him to preach the gospel to get people saved, and to enfold them in the church. If he doesn't believe that, no one but the Holy Spirit can help him! The most important step in breaking the 200 barrier is to believe that God wants to build a great church through you.

A great church's most important goal is to reach those who are without God, hopelessly and eternally lost. The billions of people who do not know Christ as their Savior, who live in the daily pain of guilt and uncertainty, call for the development and exercise of the gift of faith. If we are going to see growth in our churches, particularly beyond the 200 barrier, we must increase the measure of our faith so we can understand the work God is trying to get done in the world and believe that He wants to do that work through us and in our churches.

34

SUMMARY

- Faith is essential to church growth.

- The gift of faith (instrumental, insightful, interventional) is exercised by most church growth pastors.

- Any pastor's faith can be increased by:
    Reading about faith in the Bible
    Reading about faith in inspiring books
    Reading the stories of great churches
    Looking for examples of mountain-moving faith
    Listening to people of great faith
    Asking God to increase your faith
    Being willing to take risks

Reference Note:
    1. Elmer L. Towns, *Stepping Out on Faith* (Wheaton, Ill.: Tyndale House, 1984).

STEP 4

Set a Barrier-Breaking Goal

If you are going to break through the barrier, set a three-year goal that is well beyond the barrier and manageable within existing and available facilities. I suggest the goal be at least 300, and this small only if there is no way of handling a larger crowd in existing or available facilities. A goal of 300 is more than doubling and may appear very large if you're only running 115 to 120. I admit that there are times when doubling is not manageable, but in attempting to break the barrier, it is the only realistic goal.

One of the characteristics of a good goal is that it be realistic. That means it should be possible, with God's help, to achieve the goal. In breaking the 200 barrier, it is important to get well beyond the barrier; otherwise there is a gravity effect that tends to pull the attendance back down to or below it. You can't go to 250 and think, "Thank the Lord we made it, and now we can take time to do some other things." You must move on beyond the gravity effect.

I would not recommend, however, a goal beyond 500. It's a logical numerical point, and if you set the goal beyond

500, it will be perceived as formidable. So a realistic goal for breaking through the barrier should be somewhere between 300 and 500. If your facilities will hold 500, then set the goal for 500 even though that might be three times your present size. It takes excessive amounts of energy to get a rocket out into space. But once it gets beyond the pull of gravity, it no longer requires as much energy to sustain its flight. That's the way it works in churches. The goal must be set sufficiently beyond the barrier so there is no question about the fact that you're going to escape the gravity effect.

The three-year goal indicated earlier is based on a study of churches that actually broke the barrier. From 1976 to 1986, 27 churches in a smaller evangelical denomination grew from 150 members to over 250. Ten-year growth graphs of members, morning worship attendance, and Sunday School average attendance were plotted for all 27 churches.

A look at a few typical graphs will be helpful at this point. The bar graphs on the following pages indicate annual increases of new converts and transfers in. The losses by death and transfers out are shown below the horizontal line. The line graph shows annual membership, morning attendance, and Sunday School average attendance.

Church A broke through the barrier by growing from 150 members and attendance in 1980 to well over 250 members and attendance in 1984. Actually, morning attendance passed the 250 level a year earlier than membership. (The denomination began collecting morning worship attendance figures in the mid-'70s. Those instances in which the line descends to zero merely indicate *no report* that year and should not be considered in the growth pattern of the church.) So this church broke the barrier in three or four years, depending on how you want to count it. A look at new convert growth (in this case membership growth) reveals a sizable increase in 1983, the greatest year of morning attendance gain. That attendance increase was consolidated in

CHURCH A
Growth History

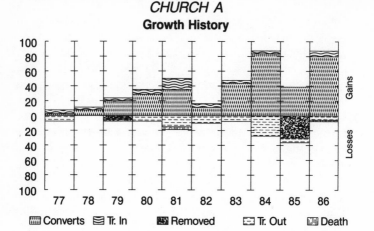

Legend: ▥ Converts ▤ Tr. In ▨ Removed ▥ Tr. Out ▥ Death

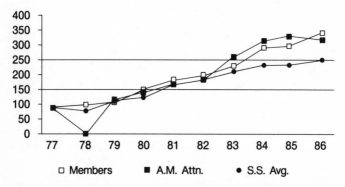

Legend: ▢ Members ■ A.M. Attn. ● S.S. Avg.

membership in 1984 with truly outstanding new convert growth. Note also the limited transfer growth.

Church B shot through the barrier in morning attendance in little more than a year. Membership to that point required three to four years. Notice the strong new convert growth between 1978 and 1982. Observe also the small number of transfers in.

Church C took only two years to pass through the barrier in both membership and morning attendance. Sunday

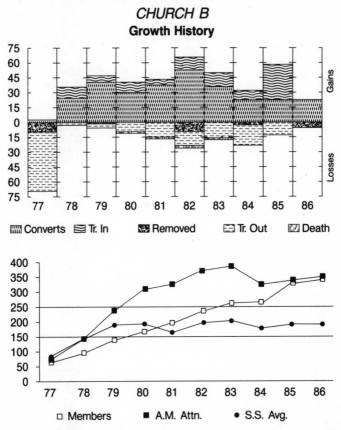

CHURCH B
Growth History

Legend: Converts · Tr. In · Removed · Tr. Out · Death

Legend: Members · A.M. Attn. · S.S. Avg.

School appears to coincide with morning attendance. Once again growth in new converts was strong as compared to transfers in. The decrease in new convert growth after 1982 resulted in a plateau. Losses by death and transfer during 1984-86 will result in significant losses in the future unless new convert gains return.

Church D coasted along at the lower limits of the barrier for many years and then exploded through it in slightly over two years in both membership and morning attendance. It is

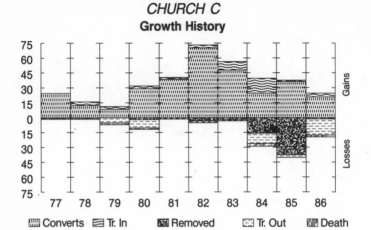

CHURCH C
Growth History

Converts | Tr. In | Removed | Tr. Out | Death

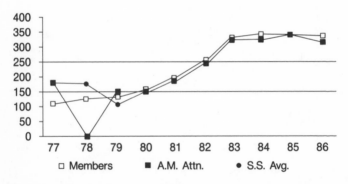

□ Members ■ A.M. Attn. ● S.S. Avg.

important to notice the change in scale on this graph. The new convert growth in 1983 would go off the chart on the previous scale. The same is true for membership and attendance on the line graph. This is probably the appropriate graph on which to observe that growth can begin at any time, even after years of nongrowth.

Church E shows a church that broke the barrier and then dropped back into the barrier zone. Notice, first of all, that it took four years to get through the barrier for membership

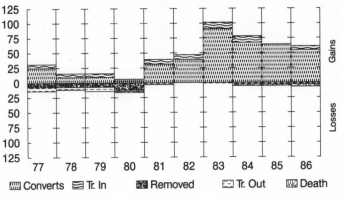

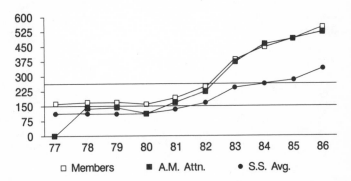

and about two for morning attendance. This graph provides an excellent example of the gravity effect. Church E didn't get far enough through the barrier to get beyond the gravity effect. Consequently, it settled down and probably will drop even lower in the future. The new convert pattern of this church is very interesting.

Church F offers another example of the necessity for breaking the barrier rapidly. It took five to six years to get through the barrier, and it appears to be trapped by the grav-

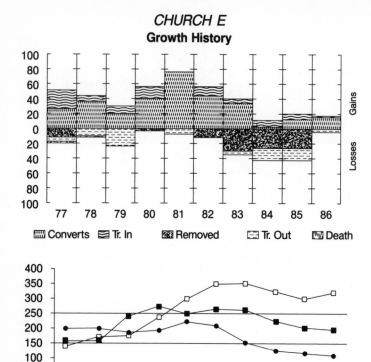

CHURCH E
Growth History

Gains / Losses

▨ Converts   ≋ Tr. In   ▨ Removed   ▤ Tr. Out   ▨ Death

□ Members   ■ A.M. Attn.   ● S.S. Avg.

ity effect. However, it is possible that in the next decade it might continue its slow growth and ultimately escape the barrier zone. But if that happens, there will have to be a dramatic turnaround in new convert growth. The prospects are not bright for Church F.

These six churches are reasonably typical of the 27 churches that broke through the barrier in the past decade. It is interesting to note that (1) the churches pierced the barrier in three years or less, (2) morning attendance normally led

CHURCH F
Growth History

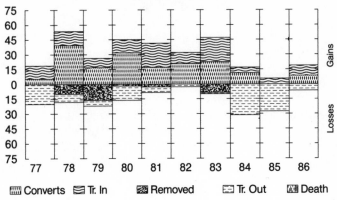

Converts Tr. In Removed Tr. Out Death

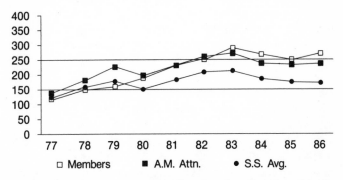

☐ Members ■ A.M. Attn. ● S.S. Avg.

membership. It was a surprising and sad reality that Sunday School almost never led the way. In fact, the single exception of all 27 churches was an ethnic congregation. (3) New convert growth is critical to breaking the barrier. The patterns indicate concerted evangelistic effort rather than consistent biological additions. (4) Transfer growth does not figure significantly in breaking the barrier. This was true in almost every instance, even in rapidly growing suburban areas. Of course, it is possible that some of the new converts should

43

have been listed as transfers in, but the uniformity of the pattern for all churches argues against that possibility.

Almost all the churches grew from below 150 members to over 250 members in three years or less. The average for all 27 churches was 2.6 years, pointing to the hypothesis that the best way to break through the 200 barrier is rapidly. There are several reasons why this is true.

Perhaps the best explanation is the power of inspiration and immediate commitment. While tenacity and persever-ance are vitally important to church growth, explosive growth seems to come from short periods of inspiration and diligent effort. There is a sense in which the Pareto principle is involved here.

Alfredo Pareto was an Italian economist who proposed the theory that 20 percent of our efforts will yield 80 percent of our results. While this is not normally thought of in terms of time, our research indicates that it may be applicable there as well. Most people are aware that they are much more productive on some days than on others. In fact, a careful analysis might reveal that approximately 80 percent of their productive work is accomplished in about 20 percent of their time. While this would undoubtedly be controversial, careful reflection could give some insight into why rapid church growth is the best way to break through the 200 barrier.

Other research reveals that districts that have multiplied new churches rapidly have done so immediately following a period of inspirational input. Most of their churches were planted in a one- to three-year period following the point of inspiration, and thereafter the number of churches planted were very few. It has led to the church multiplication theory that I call "jump in and swim for your life." Districts that plant many churches in a short period of time and then spend the next few years strengthening, consolidating, and housing those churches are much more effective in the long run than districts that make plans to plant lots of churches over a longer span of time.

44

The problem with the plan to prepare for growth in the future, to get everything in readiness, to amass the resources, and to design the strategy is that the inspiration cools off before the activity actually begins. To put it bluntly, the plan fizzles out. There just isn't enough strength in a plan. It takes inspiration to make a great plan come to completion. The adage "Do it now" applies to breaking the 200 barrier just as much as to daily discipline.

But there is another reason for planning to break the 200 barrier rapidly. When you try to break the barrier slowly, the social forces that tend to keep an organization small have time to come to bear and prevent it. When people begin to realize that they are losing control, that the relationships are changing, and that the style of ministry is changing, they begin to resist it. This may not be at the conscious level. It may be a subconscious response, but the result is the same. When you go through the barrier quickly, people don't have time to discover what is occurring until you are well beyond the barrier.

That sounds devious, but it really isn't. It's simply working with human personality the way it is. When you flood the church with new people and it's growing like gangbusters, the "controllers" and "resisters" rejoice right along with you. If you get beyond the barrier, begin your consolidation, and make the changes necessary to the new organization, you'll already be a different kind of church before there is opportunity to create waves. The church will be large enough in most instances that resistance will be futile. In fact, generally you'll already have a sufficient influx of new people on the board to tilt it toward progress.

We have talked about the need for the goal being at least 300 to overcome the gravity effect of the barrier. We have discussed the reasons for the goal being limited to a three-year period. We must now talk about setting a goal that is manageable within existing facilities.

Sociological strangulation is a church growth term that means you've run out of space to hold the people. This restriction on growth is real. Space is essential to growth. If you don't have enough, you must build or figure out another way to provide it.

Generally, in breaking the 200 barrier, conducting two services is not a very good option. You don't have enough people for two services. It has been done successfully, but more frequently it hasn't worked because it reduces the size of both groups below acceptable levels and tends to demoralize instead of to increase morale. The factor that we are dealing with here is called *critical mass*. A certain size is necessary to provide a sense of adequacy. This, of course, varies from church to church and from community to community, but going to two services in a church of approximately 200 generally violates critical mass. The problem must be solved by the unique use of existing space. Let me give you an example.

In our first pastorate, we were multiplying Sunday School classes, starting them everywhere we could. We actually started a Sunday School class at the end of the hall, and we called it the 707 Class because the chairs were arranged like the inside of a Boeing 707 airplane. (It should have been DC 9, but we didn't know the difference.) In those days there were two seats on one side of the aisle and three on the other. Boeing 707s were brand-new, and that type of seating was really uptown. It wouldn't be a good name today, but it was then. Our class at the end of the hall was successful.

To overcome limited space, you must use your facilities creatively. Clear out a storage room. You can always rent space for storage. Do not use available space for anything other than growth when you're trying to break through the barrier.

There may also be a problem with sanctuary space, and the way to resolve that is to start services in separate areas for nursery, toddlers, kindergarten church, primary church, junior church, and perhaps eventually a teen church. There are ways of dealing with sociological strangulation, but you must be imaginative.

You may be in a situation where you can rent a place across the street or go to the corner restaurant and rent rooms for Sunday morning. Your growth goal must take into consideration either the facilities that you presently have in your church structures or those available to you nearby. If going beyond the 300 barrier is impossible in present facilities, it might be advisable to wait. However, it can be dangerous to wait for adequate facilities because frequently the motivation to grow is a long time in returning.

SUMMARY

Breaking the barrier requires:

- Setting a goal well beyond the barrier, manageable within existing or available facilities.
- Setting a goal within a three-year time limit. Get beyond the gravity effect.
- Breaking through the barrier rapidly, during periods of inspiration and diligent effort.
- Making creative use of existing facilities while avoiding sociological strangulation.

STEP 5

Think Through Your Plan

It isn't necessary to plan in detail everything that is going to happen over the next several years, but it is very important to have *thought through* what's going to take place as the church grows through the barrier.

How are you going to launch the project? How will you answer your critics? (You will have critics.) How will you finance the project? (It's going to cost money.) What are you going to do when you break the barrier? Do you have the physical and emotional energy to keep the project going? Is this something you're going to do for only a year or two and then back off and catch your breath? Even though it is a matter of commitment, such a project requires that you be certain you have the physical and emotional energy to carry it to completion.

Some pastors have had growth as their goal, but when growth came, they discovered they had overextended themselves. They had neither the pastoral staff nor the lay leaders to do what needed to be done. They ran into an impossible situation so far as facilities were concerned, and they didn't know how to resolve it. They hadn't even thought about it!

You can't have all the answers—you don't know what the questions are. But you can have thought through your plan and said, "Now, here's what I think I'll do when a certain situation arises. If that doesn't work, I will be ready for the situation and do something else about it."

Don't overplan. It takes too long, consumes too much energy that can be used for growth, and it will have to be altered from time to time anyway. A plan is something you're going to do if you don't do something else. Sound foolish? It isn't. Circumstances change no matter how you plan. Nine times out of 10 the major aspects of your plan will work; but if something comes along that's more important or more significant, change your plan or modify it. The probabilities are that if you plan in great detail, much of it is going to be scrapped because you're going to discover it didn't fit what actually happened. It is sufficient to set your direction and think through your plan of action.

What will you do with 500 people? How soon will you add additional staff? Not just the third staff member, but when are you going to add the fourth, and the fifth? And how are you going to pay for all that staff? If you're like most churches, you live from hand to mouth.

What are you going to do when you have twice as many people? You're going to need a larger building. Have you thought that through? That's an important step to think about.

Thinking through your plan is not merely organizational and structural. It involves a plethora of problems that must be met and overcome. The rest of this section describes 10 problems of growth that pastors tend to overlook or underestimate.

1. *Money*

The most obvious is money. Often when a pastor projects the financial needs for growth, he greatly underestimates the cost of dramatically increased overhead. The heating bill may not increase, but janitorial expenses may escalate with the added traffic.

To take care of the increasing numbers, new and updated equipment will be required. Technological advances have provided much greater efficiency for church offices, but the price tag is not cheap. With the equipment comes the necessity for increased supplies.

And if all this isn't enough, program costs go up dramatically. It is difficult to run a growing church on the same program expenditures that were available for a smaller church.

The need for remodeling certain areas of the building as a result of growth is bound to come. Frequently enlargements to the physical plant must be made, and increased parking is required. The lot next door that the church hoped someday to purchase will have to be bought sooner than anticipated. Not that the significantly greater cost of operating a larger church isn't worth it, but pastors frequently underestimate the cost.

When we were pastoring a smaller church, we used to look at the larger churches and wonder what they did with all their money. We thought that if we just had that much income, we could do remarkable things; yet the realities are that most larger churches struggle to maintain their commitments.

Money is one of the areas in which the church board becomes very much involved, and conflicts occur over the necessity of certain expenditures. Managing growth means managing the expanding finances. It means thinking ahead to what your priorities are going to be for expenditures within a given year. It means anticipating the new program items you are going to add to the schedule and planning how you are going to finance them. It means demonstrating to your church board and to your people that you know how to allocate the funds of the church so that programs can grow and expand without taking the church into insolvency. This is why it is so vitally important for the pastor to think through his plan.

2. *Facilities*

The second problem area is facilities. Projections for housing the Sunday School are generally inadequate. It isn't easy to know how much space will be required for growth. Parking also becomes a problem. Additional land is very expensive if it is available at all. In many instances there simply are no possibilities for expansion. The only alternative is to contemplate a move.

When a move is undertaken, not only is there tradition and emotional attachment, there is also the reordering of priorities and target groups for the church. The need for facilities to house growth presses the pastor who would lead his people into expansion to think through his plan. What will growth in this locale mean and require? Do we have the emotional energy and the commitment to see it through?

3. *Staff*

The third problem that pastors tend to overlook or underestimate concerns staff. I am coming increasingly to believe that the reason many churches are not growing larger is that they are not developing a sufficient staff quickly enough. They may get one staff member and think they're very progressive when, in fact, they really should have hired two. Despite the economic factors, to move a church into the 300 to 500 category, staff must be expanded soon enough and large enough.

If the increased staff is properly deployed and supervised, they will pay for themselves. At the time of hiring, you probably need only half the necessary money. For example, if it's going to cost $30,000 to add a person to the staff, you will need to have about $15,000 available for support during the first year. Their ministry should bring in the other $15,000.

I always expected a staff person to pull about 10 couples around himself, 2 or 3 of these being families already in the church. It's only logical that some people in the church are going to relate to the new staff member and become their right-hand workers. That's fine. But beyond those I expected them to pull about 6 or 7 other couples out of our prospect list. When they do that and get them saved and contributing to the church, they're going to pay for themselves.

It needs to be plainly stated here that we are not talking about multiplying staff as an ecclesiastical status symbol. Not at all! Too many pastors think they have it made when they can hire a full-time staff person. This does not make a church a big church. And we are certainly not talking about creating staff so that the pastor doesn't have to work as hard. As every senior pastor knows, each staff person added means he works harder. You really have to keep ahead of your staff to effectively utilize them. We're talking about making it harder on the pastor, but we are talking about expanding the opportunity for the church to grow.

Staff persons should not be considered as assistant ministers who do the same things as the senior pastor at a different level, or persons to whom the leader can delegate the things he really didn't want to do. That is the wrong philosophy. The staff person should be an extension of the ministry, making it possible for the senior pastor to do more in special areas, such as youth, music, and evangelization, than he could possibly do without the additional staff. That's one perspective on staff use.

When you hire staff, volunteer people tend to say, "Thank the Lord, we finally have someone paid to do that task, and now I don't have to do it." That is a misinterpretation of reality, though it is a typical response of people who have worked in smaller churches all their lives. They have not matured in their organizational perspective to the point that they understand staff people are not hired to do their work but to help them work more effectively to reach more people and offer more services and ministries. If you don't get a staff person who understands that, you're going to have to train that person in a hurry. Generally, it's up to you to train your staff to understand what their task is, and it's very important that they in turn not allow people to back off from volunteer responsibilities.

The attitude of "We're not going to hire someone until we absolutely have to" is also self-defeating, though I once believed and accepted that philosophy. A church needs rather to ask, "What is it that needs to be done?" and "Are we at the point that someway, somehow we can hire a staff person who will enable us to move out in dramatic and effective ways of ministry?" That is a perspective I believe is workable. The smaller church of necessity may need to begin by hiring a part-time secretary and/or a part-time music director, or even using volunteers. Later these may become full-time staff persons on a paid basis. There are laypeople who really want to keep from proliferating staff, to keep the organization as small as possible. Such a nonproductive attitude needs to be overcome. Growth comes only through aggressive action and activity.

4. *The Pain of Change*

The fourth problem is the pain that people experience in change. Change is not just doing things differently. Change is not just fruit-basket turnover in personnel. Change is an experience of pain in the lives of people.

The leaders with whom they were at ease are no longer in positions of leadership. The processes they were familiar with they no longer understand. There is a general sense of confusion about how things are operating and the nature of their relationship to the Christian community. In time they will be as comfortable with the new program as they were with the old one, but for the time being they are experiencing pain.

Pastors frequently interpret this as opposition or resistance or extreme conservatism, none of which may be the case. Unless pastors accept the human nature aspect of this phenomenon, they will encounter unnecessary resistance and reaction to their leadership. As the shepherd of the sheep, the pastor who would lead his church into growth will do his best to minimize the pain and bring a sense of ease to the people.

Since there can be major difficulties in effecting change in the minds of the laymen of the church, the knowledgeable pastor will lean on the Lord for spiritual wisdom and power to bring the needed changes to pass.

5. *Personal Growth*

The fifth problem area that pastors must face is the need for personal growth. This is not simply a matter of securing more education. It is not just a matter of reading a book a week, or keeping in touch with what's going on in the community. It is considerably more basic than that. It is the need to grow, to be a better person, to be a more competent administrator, a more skillful worship leader, to improve in personal relationships, to have a greater vision for building God's kingdom, to be less reactionary and more proactive, to preach sermons that reflect a mature grappling with the issues of life, to evidence a greater sensitivity to the needs of a broader range of people, and to generally perform more competently in ministry.

While this may sound frightening, such growth is altogether possible. It depends not so much on the pastor's I.Q. as it does on his personal holiness and his willingness to learn. Opportunities for personal growth abound, and the primary reason that pastors fail to grow is not that they are unable to, but that they do not take advantage of the opportunities.

Proverbs declares that "iron sharpens iron" (Prov. 27:17). The pastor who would grow personally must bring his views and his methods under the scrutiny of astute persons in the Christian community, his peers, and those who are engaged in personal growth themselves. If his peers are also serving in growing churches, so much the better.

6. *Changing Expectations*

The sixth problem for pastors is changing expectations. A church of 400 will be a different church than a church of 200, even if the original 200 are still there. A variety of new expectations will arise around the new people. There will be different preferences in worship styles and a heightened demand for quality programming. There will be variety in musical tastes.

A pastor who thinks through his plan will take into consideration the fact that when his church grows, it will be different, and what is expected of him as a minister will be different. A subtle shift in the way the total congregation perceives the pastor will not always be understood by the older members. Newer members will not even know what the previous expectations were. The entire congregation in general will have a revised set of expectations of the pastor when the church doubles in size. They will expect greater excellence, more competent performance, and more administrative skill amid a complex set of new responsibilities.

He cannot say, "I am who I am; they'll like me as I am or not at all." Neither will he be required to deny his own identity or superimpose a sort of outgoing superficiality. Basically he must simply face the realities of growth adjustment.

7. *Opposition*

The seventh area is opposition. This, of course, may happen without growth, but it is certain to accompany growth. While by far the majority of people will be happy and pleased with growth, there are some who for one reason or another will project their discontent on the pastor.

Frequently the opposition comes from good people, even persons who are strong leaders in the church, not from those who are selfish and sinful. This sometimes occurs because they are losing control of the church, and other times because there is a conflict of values. The pastor's values with regard to growth may not correspond to the members' values with regard to relationships in the church. But whatever the circumstances, the pastor must anticipate some opposition and know how he will deal with it. Reacting and undermining a layperson to maintain his own position of leadership will compromise something very precious. There are better ways to deal with opposition.

8. *Lay Leaders*

Another hurdle to overcome is an inadequate number of lay leaders. Added to personal growth and the addition of staff is the need for a great corps of volunteer leaders. Without constant attention to developing new lay leaders, a church will run out of resources rather quickly.

The problem is not only one of quantity, it is also one of quality. An interesting phenomenon of growth is that a different level of leadership is required for leading a larger church than for leading a smaller church. Board members who were more than adequate when the church was at 200 may not be able to think as effectively for a church of 400-500. In some instances, the previous board members may be helped to grow and to think in larger terms. In other instances change will be necessary to provide ongoing leadership. Quantity itself is tremendously demanding, and the pastor must give constant attention to development of people into positions of leadership in ministries such as Sunday School classes, Bible study groups, and outreach.

9. *Small-Group Activity*

A deficiency can be seen sometimes in the lack of enough

groups to assimilate growth. This is particularly a problem for a pastor who has grown up in a smaller church or has served for an extended period in a smaller church, or one who really doesn't want a lot of activities in the church.

The only way to absorb people and guarantee that they have the necessary social relationships within the church is to make sure there are adequate groups into which these people can fit. While softball teams, basketball teams, bowling teams, and other sport activities are not particularly spiritual in nature, they are a point of entry for people with those kinds of interests.

Groups like these can be a lot of trouble, but they must not be discontinued, because they are of great value to incorporating and assimilating people into the church. The group life of the church must be multiplied greatly to effect growth. Twice as many groups will not be sufficient. It will take three, four, five, and six times as many groups as used to exist. In addition to traditional kinds of groups, study groups, mission groups, recreational groups, music groups, fellowship groups, and a multitude of other groups will be required to assimilate the people into the life of the church. The pastor must anticipate this and plan for it lest it be the pitfall that undermines all previous growth effort.

10. *Personal Demands*

The 10th and final problem that pastors generally overlook or underestimate is the problem of excessive demand for personal commitment, energy, and persistence. Leading a church in growth is not easy. It will not permit laziness nor allow an inordinate amount of recreation. In fact, it will probably be more demanding than it should be, requiring commitments that ordinarily would not be made. It will require rising early and working late as a regular schedule. Responding to impossible demands for ministry will require enormous amounts of energy, far more than the pastor anticipated when he began to lead the growth thrust. It may be tolerable the first year or the second year, and maybe even the third or fourth, but ultimately it will take its toll.

Unfortunately the pastor cannot opt to simply walk away. A dream is involved. A vision is involved. More people than the pastor are committed to this dream and vision. He cannot desert the people who believed him when he articulated the dream and declared he was willing to pay the price if they would follow him. He must find a way to preserve his health, to save his family, and to save his own soul, but he must persevere in pursuit of the dream and the vision that God gave him on the mountain, to which his people so joyfully and faithfully responded. He will stick with it when the demands become unreasonable.

When the pastor determines that he is going to lead his church to 300, 500, or beyond, he must anticipate the problems and plan how he is going to meet them, how he is going to respond to them, and how he is going to overcome them. Thinking through the plan is one of the most important steps in breaking the 200 barrier.

SUMMARY

Thinking through your plan involves looking ahead and anticipating changes without overplanning. It involves not merely organizational and structural planning, but a plethora of problems that must be met and overcome. There are 10 problems that pastors tend to overlook or underestimate when planning for church growth:

1. Money
2. Facilities
3. Staff
4. The pain of change

5. Personal growth
6. Changing expectations
7. Opposition
8. Inadequate number of lay leaders
9. Need for more small-group activity
10. Personal demands

STEP 6

Focus on the Critical Few

One of the most important aspects of breaking through the 200 barrier, particularly in a short period of time, is to concentrate your energies on only two or three activities. This recommendation follows the reasoning of the management principle called the "critical few." The Louis A. Allen's *Professional Manager's Guide* defines the critical few as follows: "In any given group of occurrences, a small number of causes will tend to give rise to the largest proportion of results" (p. 127).

Focusing on the critical few is recommended as one of the steps, not simply because it is a management principle, but because its effectiveness is easily observed in practice. This is particularly true in rapid growth. It may be a little more difficult to explain slow growth, but rapid growth can generally be accounted for by one or two activities of the church. Of course, the question is, which few activities should you concentrate on?

The suggestions that follow are a seven-point process for determining the critical few activities and assuring concentration on those activities. There is nothing profound about these seven points. In fact, they are quite simple. But if followed carefully, they should help you to grow through the 200 barrier rapidly.

1. Make a list of all the activities in which your church is presently engaged. Initially this may be a fairly long list, depending on the size of your church. The average would probably be somewhere between 10 and 25. Be sure to include fellowship activities as well as organizational activities.

Activities don't have to be structured to qualify. If the people of your church enjoy getting together informally for social fellowship, include that in the list. Include small-group activities, even some that people might call cliques. Those small groups are frequently very effective in winning new people. They also are very effective in shutting new people out. It all depends on their attitude toward growth.

Somewhere in the list, or separately, you should include the activities of the pastor. The pastor is a major resource for growth in any church. How he uses his time and energy is a critical factor in the church's growth. Be sure the list includes all outreach activities, visitation programs, community service activities, advertising programs, radio or television ministry, and any other activity that has reaching new people as its primary goal.

Such a list could be prepared in less than an hour. Using a group of people to compile the list adds a variety of perspectives. If you do not use this method, lay the list aside for a day or so and then come back to it. This should enable you to make it more comprehensive.

You may be surprised at what this list reveals to you. Most churches spend a lot of energy on activities that really do not benefit much; however, you're probably doing much better than you think. You will no doubt find that you and your church are doing many wonderful things and that your ministry is blessing and helping far more people than you realized. But don't let that mislead you either. Your objective is not only to identify all of the good and wonderful things you are doing, but to identify the critical few activities that will be most effective in helping you grow rapidly through the 200 barrier.

2. Now make another list. This time list all the activities you believe to be growth producing. It will probably be considerably shorter than the previous one. Again, you may want to include a group of people in preparing this list so you will have a variety of perspectives.

Some research will be necessary. Go to your library and locate books that describe ways to grow, or ideas to build the Sunday School. Don't be too selective. Even old, out-of-date books have many good ideas. On your first pass, write down any potential growth-producing idea, even though you are reasonably sure you would never use it in your church. A combination of ideas might spawn a tremendous growth idea for your church. This isn't your final list anyway; this is your fishing hole. You'll throw all but the biggest and the best ideas back.

While some ideas in sources from other denominations may not fit easily into your theology, you will find that most growth ideas are amazingly nondenominational, even non-independent. Most good growth ideas will fit anywhere. Don't be afraid to borrow from any source for this list of possible activities. It may take more than one pass at this project over a period of weeks to bring to it the best possibilities.

You now have two very good lists from which to work—a list of all the activities in which your church is presently engaged and a list of all the growth-producing activities you can uncover.

3. Point 3 in the process is to go through the first list and select the three to five activities that you believe are produc-

ing the best growth. It is important that this not be point 2 in your process. The reason is that the preparation of the second list will help you to understand growth-producing ideas more clearly, enabling you to select wisely when you begin to determine your own program. You will not want to choose an activity simply because someone suggests it.

It may be difficult to identify the three to five growth-producing activities in your program. You may discover that you presently have none. If possible, do a little research. If you have a new couple in your church, find out what was responsible for winning them. When you have asked several couples or individuals what influenced them to come, you will get a better picture of what is responsible for growth in your church. This is one of the most important points in the process.

It is recommended that the pastor personally reduce the list to only three to five activities, then check his results with some people whose judgment he trusts. It might even be a good idea to submit the list to a fellow pastor who understands church growth. Be careful that you do not omit from the final selection an activity that was responsible for present growth. Unless careful attention is given to point 3 in the process, it is altogether possible that such a mistake could be made.

4. You will be in less familiar territory in point 4. Out of all the great growth ideas you wrote down on list No. 2, you must choose three to five that you believe would work not just somewhere but in your specific church. You will probably ask yourself, how can I do this when I don't know what is going to work?

In selecting these programs, you must be certain you have the personnel resources and perhaps the facilities to actually implement the programs under consideration. For example, if the growth-producing idea is a recreational program, but you do not have a gymnasium or other suitable facility, you may not be able to adopt that activity. A word of caution is in order: Do not pursue some attractive idea that requires constructing a building or doing extensive remodeling of your existing facilities. This could lead you on a wild goose chase that would dissipate your energies, misdirect your efforts, and undercut your abilities to reach your goal.

There are wonderful growth ideas that might double your attendance if you only had a staff person or an educational unit or a van or something else that costs a lot of money or takes a lot of time to secure. Don't listen to the siren voices from the enchanted island of "Wouldn't it be nice if we just had something else." Be realistic and try to select activities that you can accomplish with your present resources. Do not shut off creativity, but develop innovative ways of using your existing facilities and redeploying your personnel.

Consider every possible growth activity on the list and how it might be implemented in your church. You can already imagine that this is going to be a time-consuming process. If it is done once over lightly, you will probably not make good decisions. Take a week or even two if necessary. It is not essential to include others in this process unless you feel more comfortable with their help. The important thing is to be careful and deliberate in reducing the list down to three to five growth-producing activities.

Once you have reduced the list to the approximate number, you should review the church growth books on your bookshelf. Refresh your memory about church growth principles to make sure your evaluation is properly informed with church growth concepts. You might have forgotten some factors in the process of reducing the list. When you have settled on three to five ideas, you have completed point 4 of the process.

5. Point 5, synthesis, is more than just a combination of the two lists. You must synthesize the best growth-producing ideas your church is currently engaged in with the best

growth-producing ideas your church is not presently doing. There is more to that than ending up with 6-10 growth-producing activities. The truth is that you need to reduce the list to 3-5, preferably only 3. This, of course, is the most important step in the process because it will determine the critical few activities on which you and your church will focus in the three years that lie ahead.

If your church is not presently growing and has not grown for recent months or years, you may be tempted to conclude that there is nothing on your list of present activities that is growth producing; therefore you will simply choose from the list of things that you hope will produce growth. That is a little too simplistic. Most churches are winning people even when their net attendance or membership is not increasing. An average church will lose from 5 to 10 percent of its members annually. Therefore, to remain constant after inevitable losses by death, back door, and transfer, it will have to win people back at the same rate. These gains can be significant, depending on the mobility of the community. So do not assume that because you have not had net increase in recent years, you have no growth-producing activity in your current program. Again, I would caution against eliminating a program that is perceived to be non-growth producing that might in reality be the most effective growth-producing program you have. You are concentrating on a critical few activities, not the elimination of all others.

One of the rules to keep ever before you is that *the best way to determine what will work is to look at what has worked.* We are so taken with enticing programs that we are more frequently led astray by what ought to work than we are by simple observation of what has actually worked in practice.

In most instances I would argue for a list of not more than three growth activities, but for some churches it may be more realistic to think in terms of only one or two, particularly if they do not have resources of personnel and facilities to concentrate on three.

Such a focus should expend somewhere in the range of 50 to 75 percent of the church's energies on the one or two chosen programs. Perhaps only a program as expansive as the Sunday School could actually consume that percentage of the local church's energies, so bear in mind that you must not spread yourself too thin. Hone the list of critical activities down to the least possible number.

Having completed the first five points of this scary business, you are now looking at what you will spend the major portion of your energies on for the next three years. Are you willing to spend that much of your time and effort on those two or three activities? Have you considered what a serious mistake it would be if those activities were not actually growth producing?

Arriving at the final selection requires not only wisdom but divine guidance. Don't skimp on prayer. "The arm of flesh will fail you— / Ye dare not trust your own." The first five points of the process will require, at the most, two or three months and, in fact, could be done in an intensive couple of weeks.

Now that you have actually selected what you believe are the critical few activities, there are two other important points to the process.

6. In point 6 you will detail the implementation of the critical few activities. It is one thing to determine that a visitation program is an outstanding growth activity; it is quite another to know exactly what kind of visitation program you're going to have and how it is going to be implemented in your church. If you do not have a clear plan for doing this, you may have made an incorrect selection.

At this point you may discover you do not have the resources to carry out your program, or you will find it is more difficult to get your people to accept it than you had originally imagined. Once you see how your critical few activities can be implemented and how your people can be deployed in working in those activities, then you will know whether or not you have made a correct selection.

If you jump from one program to another, you will never get one firmly instituted and implemented in your congregation. Tenacity is in order here. At the outset you must be so convinced of its worth and its value that you are willing to stick with it and make it work and see it through for the three-year period. This is why detailing the implementation must be a part of the selection process.

Such fascinating labor is almost a work of art. You can become hypnotized by the process itself and think that because you have so many different steps and pieces to the implementation process, it's bound to work. Not so. You must not overlook simple things like the amount of time it requires from your people. Two, three, or half a dozen of your hardy souls and loyal supporters will be there, no matter how long it takes, but you may not have the kind of general response from your people that is necessary to make the project succeed.

Now, if you are sure you can implement the two or three critical activities, and if you are willing to commit yourself and the major portion of your church's energies to these activities for the next three years, then you are ready to move on to point 7. This final step is critical in the total endeavor.

7. An evaluation will help you determine whether or not you are on course. After a church has gone through a process like this, they may discover, over a period of time, they have ended up doing essentially the same things they had been doing, that for all their good intentions they really have not focused on those critical few activities. Habit is a powerful determinant of action. People may meet in gather-

ings and pledge themselves to do all sorts of things but never actually do them. Point 7 builds some checkpoints into the process that will reveal whether you are actually doing what you set out to do.

If visitation is a critical activity, then determine at the end of the first month not only how many visits were made but how many people participated. You may be excited about two or three new families coming as a result of visiting, but is it true that a significant portion of the energies of the church have been expended in this visitation thrust? Have these new families been brought in simply because of the increased visitation of the pastor and one or two other members? It is possible to get so excited about the new people that you overlook the fact that visitation is not really a critical activity in your church and that less than one-half of 1 percent of the total energies of your church are being expended in this critical-few activity. While you certainly would rejoice over the new families, for whatever reason, your evaluation system must tell you how great the participation is in the activity. You would want that information not only at the end of one month, but at the end of a quarter, at the end of six months, at the end of nine months, and at the end of a year. At the end of a year, you would want to make sure that everyone understood the implementation procedure and that an increasing number of people were participating in it.

Attention and interest will increase as you allude to this, one way or another, from the pulpit, so that the people are constantly reminded of the importance and significance of the critical-few activities. Keep a record of these announcements and when they were made.

The process of focusing on the critical-few activities is not finished until you have completed all seven points of the process. Choosing a few good growth ideas is not what is meant by focusing on the critical few, but rather a very intensive and persistent effort to determine what you *are doing* and what you *could do* that would bring significant and rapid growth to your church. Following that up with good implementation procedures and an evaluation would complete the process.

Your temptation will be to dilute the critical few. There are so many good things that a church can do and so many worthwhile ways that a pastor can expend resources that the church must diligently discipline itself to focus on a critical-few growth activities. Actually doing this will be difficult, but it will produce growth in much greater numbers than you ever believed possible.

SUMMARY

Focusing on the "critical few" activities and assuring concentration on those activities will help to break the 200 barrier rapidly. A seven-point process will help the pastor to choose wisely:

1. List all the activities your church is presently engaged in.
2. List all the activities on another list that are believed to be growth producing.
3. Select from list No. 1 the three to five activities you believe are producing the *best* growth.
4. From list No. 2 choose three to five activities most workable in your particular church.
5. Synthesize the best growth-producing ideas your church is currently engaged in with the best growth-producing ideas not presently engaged in.
6. Detail the implementation of the critical few activities decided on.
7. Evaluate monthly and quarterly to determine activity production and people involvement.

STEP 7

Create Excitement

Create excitement. "Sure!" you say. "Abracadabra! What other miracle do you want me to perform?" Well, I admit, excitement is difficult to produce, but it is an important factor in getting a church growing and in sustaining growth. My son-in-law is a member of a large church, and his observation on building a large church is that you must *create* excitement. That's what he thinks he sees in his church. Some people seem to create excitement without trying. Others work with great intentionality to accomplish it. Here are 10 possible ways excitement can be created.

1. *Prayer.* A wellspring of joy, love, faith, and expectation will emit as you pray. Pray that God will bring a great sense of excitement and victory to your life and to the lives of your people that will spill over into the public services.

2. *Promote and express positive thinking.* This sparks anticipation, it supports joy, and it overcomes trouble. We're not talking about spiritual hype but about developing a positive mental attitude. Even if positive thinking is considered secu-

lar or humanistic, it works. If you think you can, you're right. If you think you can't, you're still right.

The most profound concept I learned from the positive thinking advocates is that the mind is like a field. It will grow anything you plant in it. If you plant weeds in a field, it'll grow weeds. If you plant corn, it'll grow corn. If you plant cotton, it'll grow cotton. The same is true of the mind. If you sow negative thoughts, you will reap negative thoughts. If you sow positive thoughts, you will reap the same.

I once did not believe this, but right now I'm struggling with some thought processes that are the result of conditioning I allowed years ago when I didn't think it mattered. I didn't believe those who said, "Sow a thought and reap a desire." Now, every time I intentionally, forcefully, and deliberately force out the negative thinking I allowed, and make myself think positively, I reap a wonderful harvest.

Helping people think positively is one of your pastoral tasks. As a man thinks in his heart, so is he! (See Prov. 23:7.) Ask and you will receive; seek and you will find; knock and it will be opened to you (see Matt. 7:7-8; Luke 11:9-10). These do not necessarily indicate health, wealth, and fame, but they point toward a balanced approach to life. Neither do they suggest refusing to admit that there is sorrow, heartache, sin, disease, and pain in the world. It means recognizing those problems, believing God will enable us to rise above them. Happiness in life is largely a matter of attitude. Millionaires are often miserable, while others who have barely enough to buy groceries are radiantly happy. Positive thinking is essential to creating excitement, and when pastors stand in the pulpit, they must be positive.

When I was in my first pastorate, information was sometimes funneled to me that indicated I wasn't feeding the people. That made no sense to me, because I knew I was preaching the gospel. I was into Paul like you wouldn't believe, and thought I was doing a good job! What were my critics talking about? In my second pastorate, I remember sitting in my office one day and questioning myself, "Will this sermon help anyone? Will it encourage anyone? Will it lift someone up?" I began building sermons that way and discovered immediately the difference it made. During my first pastorate I had said in effect to the people, "You brood of vipers! Who warned you to flee from the coming wrath?" (Matt. 3:7; Luke 3:7). I didn't realize how negatively based it was. Figuratively, people came crawling into church. They had been beaten down by the world and were almost ready to give up. They struggled to be in church, and they looked at me as if to say, "Preacher, do you have a good word for me today? Does God have anything to say to me about this mess I'm living in?"

In my second pastorate, I preached texts like "My grace is sufficient for you: for my power is made perfect in weakness" (2 Cor. 12:9). Some may say I compromised—stopped preaching the whole gospel. No, I still preached on hell, on the lost condition of man, on judgment. I still preached on commitment and self-denial, but not all the time. And every Sunday I asked myself those same questions to test the helpfulness of my sermons. I actually practiced making helpful statements, though at first it sounded phony to me. I was so used to admonishing people to be better and work harder for the Lord. I began saying to them, "Hey, it's wonderful to serve God. He knows all about your situation, and He will give you the strength to face it." That's what I mean by radiating from the pulpit. Accentuate the positive.

3. *Encourage enthusiasm.* It lifts people's spirits. It's catching. Be genuine, but be enthusiastic. I learned from Dr. Curtis Smith that when you're going to the pulpit, you should get there in a hurry and act like it's worth being there. I see pastors saunter to the pulpit like they dreaded it. If you're going to create excitement, you *must* be enthusiastic and speak with enthusiasm.

"Well," you say, "that's not me." Then be as enthusiastic as you can. Obviously some people are so enthusiastic they are bouncing off the wall. You don't have to be like them, but you can be positive and speak with as much enthusiasm as you can possibly generate.

My first experience with a superchurch was at Calvary Temple, an independent congregation in Denver, in 1957. At that time, only two churches in my denomination had more than 1,000 members, and there probably weren't 50 super-churches in any denomination in America. When I asked about the secret of Calvary Temple's growth, I was told that it was the enthusiasm of the people.

—They were excited about their church.

—They recommended it to their friends.

That was over 30 years ago, when the church growth movement was only two years old. Donald McGavran's book *The Bridges of God,* which launched the movement, had just been published and was the *only* book on the subject. Now, three decades and hundreds of books later, the best explanation for outstanding church growth is *still* the enthusiasm of people about their church.

Some people consider enthusiasm a worldly and insincere emotion. Actually, the opposite is true. The two Greek words used for enthusiasm mean *God inside you.* What better source of enthusiasm is there than God inside you?

Dr. Phineas F. Bresee declared, "If any man loses his enthusiasm, he might as well be buried." He knew that a lack of enthusiasm "is one of the greatest hindrances to the work of God." He even said a lack of enthusiasm "is sure evidence that the heavenly vision is dim."

The truth is that enthusiasm is simply faith in action. It is the logical expression of the joyful knowledge of God's good news for the world.

Ralph Waldo Emerson insisted that "every great and commanding movement in the annals of the world is the triumph of enthusiasm. Nothing great was ever achieved without it."

Every superchurch is the triumph of the enthusiasm of its people.

4. *Set realistic goals.* Make them challenging but possible. A good goal will require special effort and divine help, but if it is impossible, it will discourage people instead of exciting them. A goal gives people something to get excited about. Most people want to attempt the extraordinary, and they get excited about the possibilities of achieving it.

5. *Spiritualize the work of the church* in your communication to people. In your promotion from the pulpit and in newsletters, communicate to your people that saving souls and rebuilding lives is what the work of the church is all about. You are not just increasing numbers or erecting buildings, you are doing God's work. Read the newsletters of exciting churches, and you will discover that everything is spiritually oriented. They don't just raise money. They ask their people to make a great gift to God. They aren't merely constructing a building, they are providing a place for people who are going to be won as a result of faithful stewardship. They could say, "You owe 10 percent of your income to the Lord, and you ought to give another 5 percent to help us do some of the things we're trying to do as a church," and people would say, "We can't do it. We have too many personal bills." But if you say to them, "We're doing a great work for God, and you have a chance to share in this tremendous ministry; you can make an investment in the kingdom of God," then they'll do it. Learn the secret of spiritualizing the work of the church. Is that honest? Yes, it is. The Bible says to do everything you do to the glory of God.

6. *Celebrate victories and successes.* This is extremely important. Every time someone gets saved, give it special attention in the public services. Every time someone has an answer

to prayer that is significant, report it in a public service and in the newsletter. Help the people to feel something's happening at their church, that something wonderful is going on all the time.

7. *Focus on people's needs and help them.* I venture to say that most of those attending your church would be impressed if they knew the church was actually helping people, whether it was by providing meals, giving them clothes, or helping them through problems. This is where love, acceptance, and forgiveness are important. You don't have to condone their problems or their sins, but you do need to love people. You do need to accept them just as they are, and you do need to forgive them for their wrongdoing. When you focus on people's needs, you'll discover that even the folk who never want the church to do anything except preach the gospel will be impressed that their church is really helping people.

8. *Plan outstanding programs.* We have the makings of boredom in our churches. The makings of monotony and boredom are there because we have 52 Sunday morning services, 52 Sunday night services, and 52 Wednesday night services when we do about the same things with the same people. That can get boring. So plan some outstanding programs.

Plan a musical, or something that's really big and new, and that challenges the folk to get other people involved in doing something different. We used to create excitement in my church by adding variety. People would say our church services were never the same twice. Not everyone can handle variety, but do something to give the people a feeling of expectancy.

9. *Develop inspiring worship services.* This doesn't necessarily require an emotional response in the form of outward demonstration, but worshipers should feel something. It

must fit your personality, and it has to fit your people. It should also fit within your resources. If you have someone who can "sing the glory down," great! If not, you must do something else.

10. Secure renowned guest speakers and singers from time to time. You may need to grow before you can incorporate them into your program in significant measure, but you will need to do it to maintain excitement in your church.

Surely 1 or 2 among these 10 methods will help you build excitement. It will be worth your best efforts. Nothing is so exciting as unsaved people coming to your church and being won to the Lord.

SUMMARY

Create excitement in your church by:

1. Praying until it spills over into your services
2. Thinking positively
3. Encouraging enthusiasm
4. Setting realistic goals
5. Communicating its spiritual purpose and function
6. Celebrating victories and successes publicly
7. Focusing on people's needs and helping them
8. Planning outstanding programs and services
9. Developing inspiring worship services
10. Securing guest speakers and singers for interest and variety

STEP 8

Launch a Growth Thrust

Launch a vigorous and rapid growth thrust aimed toward breaking the barrier. We have already talked about rapid growth, and we've talked about focusing in on the critical few. Now we will consider the actual launching of a vigorous and rapid growth thrust.

People love the excitement of growth and the conversion of new people. It is important to take advantage of that excitement and, I repeat, to get through the barrier before the pioneers and power structure realize what is happening to the fellowship patterns, leadership roles, and styles of ministry. Launching a vigorous and rapid growth program is critical to barrier breaking.

When you set up a three-year plan, arrange it so the first year begins in the fall or spring growth seasons, not in summer or winter. Pull out all the stops and, whatever you plan for growth, choose a method that yields rapid response. I suggest four categories of ideas for rapid growth.

One-Day Attendance Drives

While one-day attendance drives do not yield the kind of continuing results we like to see, they are a good way to shake loose some growth. The key to any kind of growth is a systematic and effective follow-up program. This cannot be just a contact program, but a program of incorporation, making sure people form close friendships within the church that will keep them tied into the fellowship through the months and years that follow.

One of the classic ideas for rapidly reaching sizable numbers of new people is the Giant Visitors' Day by Elwood Munger. He went into local churches and within one week's time doubled or tripled their attendance on Giant Visitors' Day. It was amazingly successful, but the result of the program was generally the same: Attendance declined to previous levels in succeeding Sundays. It was hoped that once people were inside the church, something would appeal to them and bring them back. But it didn't work that way. Church growth research later told us why. People do not remain in a church unless they form friendships and meaningful associations within that church. One-time exposure is not enough. That doesn't mean the Giant Visitors' Day wasn't a great idea. It means churches were not prepared at that point to capitalize on it. Properly used, it is a great rapid growth idea.

Similar methods, employed with some success, drew heavy criticism because of the embarrassing techniques involved. Unfortunately we failed to see the tremendous potential in these methods, and we threw the baby out with the bathwater. Had we known how to capitalize on them, we could have turned those methodologies into outstanding growth for our churches. In recent years, the Giant Visitors' Day has been reintroduced as Friendship Day, with up-to-date methods and more acceptable procedures. Beacon Hill

Press of Kansas City carries materials for Friendship Day. As the name change implies, the focus is now on building friendships. Another such program is available from Win Arn's Institute for American Church Growth in Pasadena, Calif. A third is available from Elmer Towns, well known in the Sunday School movement and more recently in the church growth movement. Each of these notebooks provides complete plans for a special day in which many people can be brought into the church. This is what is needed to make these one-day events effective.

Another idea, old but workable, is Fill a Pew Sunday. The success of this program depends both on the excitement generated and on the organization and involvement of a sizable number of people in the congregation. It must be remembered, however, that unless there is careful follow-up, the yield of new prospects will not be great.

A third idea for one-day attendance drives is to schedule a well-known guest singer or speaker. Musicians will generally draw better crowds than speakers unless the speaker is nationally known. If carefully advertised and planned, a good musical group will usually ensure a packed house. Some say this draws only people who go from church to church to hear musicians sing but does not really produce prospects. This is partly true. However, if a visitor's card is secured on every person attending the performance and careful follow-up is done, these one-day musical events usually yield some good prospects. It has been my observation that few churches scheduling visiting musical groups even attempt to get visitors to fill out cards. When this is overlooked, the growth value of having a guest singer is almost zero.

A fourth method for a one-day attendance drive is comparatively new in application to the church, though it is widely used in business circles. It is telemarketing. In the West, where it was used to plant new churches, it produced first Sunday attendances of 100-300, depending on the number of telephone contacts made. It has also been used in one-day attendance drives for existing churches. Basically it requires 30,000 to 50,000 phone calls to people in the community. This is a sizable task, but it can reap remarkable results. Of course, there must be a compelling reason for the people to attend. Careful preparations for following up on those who attend will inevitably secure some church prospects.

If you can get a large number of new people to visit your church in a short period of time and adequately follow up on them, you can break loose and gain momentum. That's what you need to rapidly move through the 200 barrier.

Sunday School Renewal

A second category of ideas for rapid church growth (in order to break quickly through the barrier) is Sunday School renewal. This may not seem like a rapid growth method, but I am firmly convinced that a new commitment to the Sunday School as the basic structure of the church for social incorporation and Bible instruction will produce rapid growth for many churches. Sunday School attendance in most churches is down, and there's a lot of pessimism about its growth potential, but one of the problems is inadequate commitment. For some reason, people do not recognize that the Sunday School is the only organizational unit that most churches have and the principal means of incorporating people socially into the life of the church. When that is given up, serious problems result. Continuing decline and ineffectiveness of the Sunday School is augmented by the malaise in administration, and very little is happening in prospect and absentee visitation.

What is not taken into consideration is how we are going to provide Christian training for young families in the future if we give up on the Sunday School. It cannot be carefully and systematically done from the pulpit. It cannot be comprehensively done by Bible study groups. We desperately need the Sunday School. A new commitment to it would see a rapid rise in attendance.

One of the first expressions of a new commitment to the Sunday School should be the addition of new classes, which not only releases new leaders but also provides new groups for the incorporation of visitors and prospects. One of the reasons why attendance almost always declines following an attendance drive or a fall or spring attendance increase is that usually no new structures for incorporation are created to contain the people who are reached during those growth periods. Starting new Sunday School classes is a wonderful way of incorporating the new people.

In staffing the Sunday School, leaders must revitalize the worker recruitment and training processes. Recruitment must be intensified, and the method will have to become more sophisticated. Greater attention must be given to training workers, and a better quality of training must be provided. Part of the task of renewal is providing the necessary funding and personnel resources for the training. It must be up-to-date, and it must be persistent.

Presently a "shadow boom" or an "echo boom" to the baby boom is beginning to pass through the population. Baby boomers are now parents of children who are in grade school. This offers a tremendous opportunity for growth in the Sunday School Kindergarten and Primary departments. Careful attention should be given to developing workers in these areas of the Sunday School. Unused classrooms should be reopened, painted, decorated, and prepared for the echo boom.

Careful, systematic, and committed attention to the Sunday School will provide rapid growth for many, if not most, churches. This has been true across the years, and it is still valid for thousands of churches in America today.

Visitation Blitz

A third rapid growth method for piercing the barrier is a visitation blitz. Nothing, absolutely nothing, is more effective than a face-to-face invitation. Admittedly visitation is problematic these days. In urban settings people are fearful of unfamiliar persons who ring their doorbells, especially in the evening. But we must keep in mind that great churches have been built on door-to-door visitation, and many say that even today it is still the best method for reaching people. It is widely practiced by growing churches and strongly recommended by most growth pastors.

Door-to-door visitation may be a survey. There are several that include questions like, "What don't you like about the church?" Using this indirect approach, surveyors are able to determine the kind of church people really would like to attend.

The Salvation Questionnaire (Beacon Hill Press of Kansas City) is surprisingly effective. This survey can open many doors that might otherwise remain closed.

If you don't like the survey approach to door-to-door visitation, you might want to try what has been called the farming approach. The basic idea is to go back again and again, perhaps as many as seven or eight times, cultivating the soil and ultimately looking for a harvest.

Door-to-door visitation can be effective, but the best prospect your church has is the person who has visited recently. It is important to personally contact a visitor quickly. Church growth research indicates that about 85 percent of the visitors return if they have been contacted within 36 hours of their first visit (*To Spread the Power,* by George G. Hunter III, Abingdon Press, 1987). Of course one contact is not enough. Careful and systematic effort should be exerted to get the prospects acquainted with people in the church and to establish relationships that will help them become responsible church members. There is very little activity that will yield better results than promptly following up on all of the people who visit your church.

In any visitation blitz, we must include absentee visitation, especially in view of our sizable membership losses. On an average, a church loses two out of three of the new converts they win. Sometimes the reason we lose people is conflict. More frequently they simply drift away because they were never assimilated into the heart and life of the church. Many of them explain, "We just never really felt we were a part of the church." Unfortunately, by the time the church gets around to finding out why they left, these people are generally too far gone to consider returning. Absentee visitation could help tremendously in preventing these kinds of losses.

Personal evangelism as a visitation method is particularly effective at the point of decision making. The Evangelism Explosion method has repeatedly proven that people can be led to a decision to accept Jesus Christ as their Savior through visitation. It is essential that it be tied into a social incorporation process. People are spiritual beings, but they also are physical beings with social needs. Church growth research has revealed that if we are to keep people in the church, we must socially incorporate them. Friendships developed within the church will strengthen the effectiveness of personal evangelism visitation.

Most churches, regardless of size, have people with spiritual gifts necessary for both evangelism and incorporation. Just one person with the ability to present the plan of salvation and ask people to make a decision for Christ can win as many people as all others in the church can incorporate. Those who have the gifts of hospitality, helps, service, and teaching must accept the responsibility of incorporating new converts won through this method of visitation.

While a visitation blitz may sound like a good idea, it

takes a great deal of commitment and huge amounts of energy. It requires good organization and careful record keeping. Most churches find it more work than they are willing to do, yet it remains the most effective method known for growth.

Bus Ministry

Bus ministry is another means of rapidly breaking through the growth barrier. To this suggestion a number of objections will immediately be raised. I can't say that I disagree with them. I only say that the objections do not change the reality. Of course there are problems: maintenance of the buses, staffing, unsupervised children and the problems they create in the church. These and many other problems are part and parcel of a bus ministry, but it is still a very good way to reach a large number of children quickly.

Some of the great churches of America have been built on bus ministry. Most of these would testify that with proper follow-up many parents can be reached also.

As a good, long-term ministry, hundreds of children who ride the bus to Sunday School return in their adult years because they consider that church their church.

There are many other effective ways of reaching new people. These selected methods have been chosen because they usually yield results more rapidly than others, which is the particular focus of this step.

SUMMARY

Vigorous growth aimed at breaking the barrier should begin in the fall or spring growth seasons and can be achieved in several ways. Four rapid growth ideas are:

1. One-day attendance drives
   a. Visitors Day (Friendship Day)
   b. Fill a Pew Sunday
   c. Musical events
   d. Telemarketing
2. Sunday School renewal
   A new commitment to the Sunday School as the only organizational unit in most churches and the principal means of incorporating people socially into the life of the church
3. Visitation blitz
   By far the most effective method, it takes commitment, energy, good organization, and careful record keeping.
   a. Door to door
   b. Follow-up on visitors and absentees
   c. Personal evangelism (especially effective at the point of decision making)
   d. Friendship evangelism to incorporate and assimilate
4. Bus ministry
   Results override objections when proper follow-up is employed.

STEP 9

Evangelize First

Break the barrier! Flood the church with new people and work on consolidation afterward. You may think you need to have all of your consolidation programs in place before you break the barrier, but you won't be able to do that. Go for growth! Turn all your energies toward getting scores of people from your prospect list into the church. Enroll them in your Sunday School and in your group-life structure. After that you can train workers, bring stronger leaders into the system, expand the staff, enlarge facilities, and proliferate program around the scores of new people.

Across the years I've been told we need to educate our people in how to win souls and to disciple them so they will be spiritually capable of winning a soul. That makes sense, and I believed it for several years, but it finally dawned on me that education seldom produces evangelism. Rather, evangelism makes education necessary. You can train people, educate and disciple them for years, but that won't motivate them to actually win a soul to Christ. As someone said about soul winning,

We've all read a book by Truett.
Now we know how,
But we still won't do it.

That's what you're up against. People will learn how to be soul winners but never go and win souls.

Church growth is messy. If you evangelize and win new converts into your church, you will be forced to educate them. When the new converts are seen walking up the steps of the church, stomping out their cigarettes on the front porch; when they begin talking about their life-style in the fellowship groups, people are going to say, "We must get something going for these new converts. We need to train these folk in Christian ethics. They need to know the Bible better. We must have a class for them."

The existence of new converts gives you a reason to train. Becoming a better disciple doesn't adequately motivate you to go out and make new converts. So it's important to flood the church with new people and then convert and disciple them. If you don't, you'll lose them. It's time to develop group life, train workers, expand staff, enlarge facilities, proliferate program when you have a significant increase in people.

Evangelism and education are not the only two polarities in dynamic tension with which the church growth pastor must deal. When a pastor leads his church in growth, he will face the quantity-versus-quality conflict.

There is much to be said in favor of quality. The very nature of Christianity favors an emphasis on quality. The redeeming work of Christ and the holiness of God appeal for quality. Increasing in size usually generates interest in quality, and church members who six months earlier were excited about quantity suddenly become interested in quality. The old adage "Anything worth doing is worth doing right" begins to be frequently heard.

Certainly a church should have quality services and quality concerns for people, but sometimes it is difficult to simultaneously generate both quality and quantity. The pursuit of quality expends energy that could be spent in increasing quantity.

The polarization may be even more significant. There may be something in the very nature of quality that tends to militate against quantity. But whatever realities relate to the polarization, the church growth pastor must prioritize quantity when he is trying to get the church through the 200 barrier as rapidly as possible. Unless he focuses on quantity, there really won't be any additional growth on which to improve quality. Opportunity to improve quality will come in due time.

There will be people in the congregation who simply cannot accept any priority other than quality. This conflict will be expressed in a variety of ways—in the Sunday School when it is necessary to share classrooms, or when less-than-adequate teachers are all that is available, or when there aren't enough materials or supplies for the new children in the classes. All of these situations can be corrected in time, but growth must be gained while it is possible and in sufficient numbers to carry you through the barrier. The pastor will have to assure the people that adequate emphasis on quality will be launched at the appropriate time.

A third dynamic tension involves people and facilities. Frequently a church growth pastor faces the fact that he cannot grow without facilities, nor can facilities be provided without additional people. In this circumstance, he must place the focus on increasing the number of people and deal creatively with the facilities problem. It takes considerably longer to provide facilities than is usually contemplated, and a maximum of energy and effort must be exerted to construct a building. Growth momentum will be lost in the milieu. A building may be needed, and it may be needed as soon as possible; but during the time of breaking through the 200 barrier, the emphasis should be upon reaching and winning people. These new people will then become part and parcel of the excitement engendered by the building plans.

The tension between having enough facilities to hold the growth and having enough people to pay for the additional facilities favors winning new people; however, there may be situations in which this is an absolutely impossible option. In some cases, if the church is to increase in numbers at all, it must have additional facilities. In these instances, the pastor must simply do the best he can to keep the growth momentum going while adequate leadership is given to the building program. It must be kept in mind that if it takes longer than three years to break through the 200 barrier, their chances for making it through are seriously diminished. Anything that tends to slow down the growth process must be resisted, regardless of how essential it appears.

A similar tension exists between having enough money to provide the staff essential to growth and having enough staff to provide the growth to produce the money. Particularly in the early days, the pastor seeking church growth usually faces limited financial resources. Though it is normally recommended that he hire the staff and depend on them to win new people so additional money will be given, many churches have been forced to cut back staff to part-time or terminate them altogether because there was not enough money to pay them after they were hired. This happens when growth has not occurred. Frequently people assume growth will be automatic with the hiring of additional staff. When their focus on growth dwindles, growth slackens, money becomes scarce, and the staff is an excessive financial drain on the church treasury.

The church growth pastor must deal with this tension by

using sound financial judgment concurrently with adequate staff for growth. The staff must be adequately trained and sufficiently competent in their tasks to motivate and deploy volunteers in the growth thrust. Where this happens, involved laypeople are caught up in the excitement of growth, and the staff-versus-money tension can be managed.

That brings up the final tension—between growth and morale. Does growth produce morale, or morale produce growth? There is general agreement that if you have good morale, almost anything you do will work. Conversely, if you do not have morale, much of what you attempt will be unsuccessful. It is easier to create growth than morale, and even if morale is generated, it will be fragile unless it is supported by growth. Morale is the heady feeling one gets from the sweet smell of success. "Nothing succeeds like success." A growing church will create morale, and morale will generate growth.

Balancing these tensions is an important part of flooding the church with people and then trying to consolidate the gains. The church growth pastor must keep the emphasis on growth, quantity, and evangelism while simultaneously giving attention to morale, quality, and education. The idea is not to disregard discipling, but to do it when you most need it. There should be a plan for starting new groups as the church wins new people. The same is true for enlarging facilities and expanding programs as growth occurs.

Step 9, in summary, is: Focus your efforts on winning people rather than pursuing other activities with the hope that they will win people. Evangelize first, since it is easier to get the church to accept growth plans when it is actually growing. Flood the church with new people, and then work on consolidation after you've broken the barrier.

SUMMARY

- In the process of breaking the barrier, the pastor must deal with several polarities in dynamic tension:

  Evangelism vs. education
  Quantity vs. quality
  People vs. facilities
  Money vs. staff
  Growth vs. morale

- The church growth pastor must keep the emphasis on growth, quantity, and evangelism while simultaneously giving attention to morale, quality, and education.

- Efforts should focus on winning people. Evangelize first, since it is easier to get the church to accept growth plans when it is actually growing. Flood the church with new people, then work on consolidation after the barrier is broken.

STEP **10**

Lead the Change

The pastor must be a change agent, not just in the revolu-
tionary sense, but in development and in coordination and
control of balance in the organization while it undergoes
change. It is frequently said, "Pastor, you are the key." Any-
time we want to get right down to rock-bottom responsibility,
we declare it's all a matter of leadership. Perhaps it is an
oversimplification to say that success depends on the pastor,
but it does highlight the critical importance of the church's
human leader.

A growth-oriented pastor has the ability to organize and
administer the church so the focus is on outreach and evangelism and *on meeting the needs of people.* It isn't necessarily
that he's a gifted singer or preacher, although both of those
may figure significantly, nor is it that he has a winsome personality. It's rather that he has a knack for coordinating
growth, for meeting people's needs, for making sure the
things that need to happen in that congregation actually happen.

As I visit churches, I frequently hear a growth-oriented

pastor say, "Excuse me a minute." He'll pick up the phone and call someone. I'll hear him say something like this, "Will you check on Charles and Mary? Is someone going to be picking them up for the service, or is someone going to be taking a meal over there to them?" What he is doing is taking care of the needs of the people in that congregation. If you ask him how important detail like that is to growth, he will probably say it is not very important.

Instead, he will tell you he prays a lot. He will tell you he keeps the focus on great public services. But the facts are, he instinctively knows that people's needs must be met, and he makes sure those needs are taken care of. That is real church growth leadership—the kind a pastor must provide if he is to pilot his church through the changes necessary to break the 200 barrier. At least six concepts are involved in giving leadership to this kind of change.

1. *You must have a firm resolve to change regardless of the price.* If you don't have that kind of commitment, you'll discover the price is too high, and you'll back off. You must be firmly convinced in your mind that the church must change from the ingrown concept of one big, happy family to an evangelistic organization—not to satisfy anyone's ego, but that souls will be saved. Change may be the only alternative if you are going to evangelize your community. Make a firm resolve to change.

2. *Realize that all change is perceived as pain.* Until I realized this fact of human nature, I had a lot of trouble with people who didn't want to change. I loved change, especially when people were changing to fit my preferences. It took me a long time to learn that all change is painful. Not all change brings the same degree of pain, but it's still painful, and you have to understand that to control it. People are not just hardheaded, resisting change because they are traditionalists. You have created great discomfort in their lives. If they could

be objective about it, like you are, it wouldn't bother them, but they can't. They are human beings, and you've torn up something that was very comfortable for them, and they are in pain.

3. *Keep the people willing to endure the pain for the gain.* Say to them, "I know this is very inconvenient for you, but we're doing it for Jesus' sake. We're winning souls. Here are John and Mary Smith, who were saved last week in their homes because you made this sacrifice."

In one of my pastorates we had Sunday School classes in a building nearly 200 yards away. I had to constantly say to those people, "Thank you for going to that other building for Sunday School class. I know it would have been much easier to stay here in the comfort of this building, but we're able to reach many more people because of your willingness to inconvenience yourselves." My gratitude was sincere. My people were willing to endure the pain for the gain.

To keep the goal before them lessens the pain. Spiritualize the goal and celebrate the victories.

4. *Lead the thrust to reach new people.* One of the most important aspects of controlling the change is the pastor's leadership. After the barrier has been broken, he can modify his role somewhat, but until significant growth actually occurs, he must lead the thrust and be a fellow worker with the people.

5. *Take care of people.* See that prospects are visited and drawn into a group circle. Introduce intentionality into the entire social incorporation aspect of the evangelism process. Don't wait for visitors and prospects to find friends. Create settings in which it will happen easily. Remember, people aren't looking for a friendly church, they are looking for a friend.

6. *Expand the organization and administration to make*

continued growth possible. This requires more staff, more groups, more programs, more ministries, more training, more facilities. One of the reasons we encounter numerical barriers is that we assume, since the organization and administration we've had in the past have served us well, they will also be good enough for the future. That is a faulty assumption. We must constantly keep expanding the organization. Some of the fastest-growing churches in America start a new Sunday School class every week. Think of that!

Growing churches generally add a new staff member for every 100 people. Someone may ask, "Won't we ever get done?" Not as long as you're growing. People will complain that they are out of breath. They probably always will be, but if you stop to catch your breath, you'll stop growing. If you're going to keep growing, you must keep expanding.

You may say we won 50 new converts last year. Do we have to win 60 this year? Yes, if you want to grow. And probably next year it'll be 70. You say, "There's a limit to what I can do." That's right. And each has to find his own limit, what he is willing to do, and what his vision is. That's in the law of things. You're either growing or you're dying. The Lord be thanked, there are ways of growing.

The point I'm trying to make is that the pastor must give leadership to all this change—the change from being restricted to a one-big-happy-family kind of church to becoming an outward-looking organization that can ensure that a complex variety of congregational needs are met. This is as important from a functional point of view as praying is from a spiritual point of view. Leadership generates, integrates, and facilitates growth to a remarkable extent. The pastor who plans for his church to break the 200 barrier must give thought and commitment to his own leadership development.

SUMMARY

If the pastor is to pilot his church through the changes necessary to break the 200 barrier, he must:

1. Have a firm resolve to change regardless of the price.
2. Realize that change is painful for the people in his church.
3. Keep the people willing to endure the pain for the gain.
4. Lead the thrust to reach new people.
5. Take care of people—be sensitive to their needs.
6. Expand the organization and administration to make possible continued growth.

CONCLUSION

You Can

If you are not now saying, "I have never been more enthused about breaking the 200 barrier in my church. I can't wait to get started on the steps outlined in this book," you are probably somewhere between that position and one that says, "I have read through these 10 steps, and I believe in the concepts presented, but I do not feel I have the gift of faith or the ability to overcome my own and my church's inadequacies. The hurdles are too high and too many to break the 200 barrier!"

Wherever you fall between those two attitudes, I want to encourage you to go for it anyway. Making an attempt is in itself a step toward success. The illustrious Teddy Roosevelt declared, "Far better it is to dare mighty things, to win glorious triumphs, even though checkered by failure, than to take rank with those poor spirits who neither enjoy much nor suffer much, because they live in the gray twilight that knows not victory nor defeat."

That is especially true in the work of God's kingdom. Any spiritual venture requires that we trust God for enablement, whatever our gifts or abilities. The truth is you *can* lead your church in breaking the 200 barrier. You won't coast through it, and you won't slip through it, but at this point you will have already committed yourself to intensive, intentional effort. And if your church is in the 100-150 category, you probably have all the material and human resources necessary.

The factors leading to growth are elusive. Though generally explained in terms of leadership, identifying the characteristics of leadership is almost as difficult as explaining growth. Many are convinced that one either is born with leadership qualities or else will never have them. That may be true of most great leaders, but there is also evidence that such qualities can be developed. Great gifts of leadership are not so important as enthusiasm, persistence, and attention to detail. You can manage these.

The pastor who intends to lead the church through the 200 barrier must be ready to settle for hard work, but a buoyant spirit will go a long way toward lightening the load. In this assignment vibrancy of spirit is needed, and it will come as you see the evidence of God's moving in response to your plans and prayers. If the pastor must force himself to be optimistic and to act enthusiastically, then God will help him to do that too. Optimism, enthusiasm, and spiritual vigor will be integrated into a radiance that will appeal to those who observe what is happening.

Even though the barrier must be broken within a three-year period, it will not appear overnight. There will be setbacks. It will sometimes look impossible. But if you refuse to be discouraged and persistently pursue your goal, you will almost certainly overcome the obstacles and experience success.

Persistence will be more than just hanging on. It will be an attention to detail that ensures the job will get done and the goals will be reached. This need not become a laborious involvement in administrivia, but it must include a regular checking of all the factors that require attention in the growth process. The pastor may not be directly involved in the performance of these responsibilities, but he must see that those who are so involved actually get the job done. People often do not do what is expected, but they usually do what is inspected. Make certain that tasks related to growth get done.

The 10 steps to breaking the 200 barrier, with their many subparts, may appear very complex, but the task is certainly manageable. It is a bit like building a grandfather clock. A scary presentiment rattles your self-confidence around as you look at the picture of the finished product, but each part, put in its place separately and in order, makes the task manageable.

You can do it. Go for it!